Learning About Dogs

Clicker Gundog

Helen Phillips

A LEVEL 3 Book
CLICKER TRAINERS
COURSE

Printed in the U.S. and distributed by
Karen Pryor ClickerTraining and Sunshine Books
49 River Street, Waltham, MA 02453
www.clickertraining.com
Sales: U.S. Toll Free 800-472-5425
781-398-0754

First published in 2006

Learning About Dogs Limited

PO Box 13, Chipping Campden, Glos, GL55 6WX. UK

pictures by Chris Phillips, Amy Shaler and the Author

ISBN 1-890948-30-6

Books in the Clicker Trainers Course series by Kay Laurence:

Clicker Foundation Trainer Level 1

Clicker Novice Trainer Level 2

Book of Challenges for Foundation & Novice trainers

Clicker Intermediate Trainer Level 3

Recipe books for specialised interests:

Clicker Dances with Dogs

Clicker World Obedience Training

and:

Clicker Agility for Fun & Fitness by Diana Bird

Click for Grooming, Handling and Treatment by Karen McCarthy

Interactive training games: Gena & GenAbacab

Teaching Dogs Magazine for up to date news on clicker training

www.clickertraining.com

CONTENTS

1 INTRODUCTION 1

2 FOUNDATION TRAINING **23**
 1   Introduction to the Gun 28
 2   Recall for puppies 30
 3   Target Hand 32
 4   Elastic Recall 34
 5   Sit in Front 36
 6   Positioning the dog 38
 7   Chin to hand target 38
 8   Shaking on Cue 40
 9   Jumping 42
 10 Working at a distance 44
 11 The Drop .45
 12 The Stop .47
 13 Left and right 50
 14 Back 51

3 CONTROL TRAINING **53**
 15 Capturing scent 62
 16 Teaching the dog to focus on you 66
 17 Squeal, means join me 68
 18 Measuring fitness and excitement 69
 19 Measuring effect of stimuli 71
 20 Testing control against the environment .72
 21 Using target hand to measure control . .74
 22 Using caged birds to develop
     self-control and stimulus control 75
 23 Down stay 77
 24 Sit stay 77
 25 Loose lead walking 79
 26 Using food to teach self control 81
 27 Park the dog 82
 28 Walking Free 83

4 HUNT TRAINING **85**
 29 Introducing the dog to game 96

 30 Catch up game 96
 31 Experiencing the moment 97
 32 Wing hunting game 98
 33 Hunting "Go Find" 100
 34 Hunting Placed Food 102
 35 Using cold game or scented dummy . . .103
 36 Connecting scent and location of game .105
 37 Using caged birds and quartering 108
 38 Strengthening the point with a wing 110
 39 Strengthening the point with caged bird .111
 40 Flushing on cue 112
 41 Drop to flush 113
 42 Establishing the quartering distance 115

5 RETRIEVE TRAINING **119**
 43 Retrieve assessment 120
 44 Sit and mark 122
 45 Marking from the shot 125
 46 Collection and delivery 127
 47 Generalise dummies and game 130
 48 Adding the cues 131
 49 More shaping on the pick up 131
 50 Change to hand 133
 51 Which way to deliver 134
 52 The complete chain 136
 53 Directed retrieve 139
 54 Blind Retrieve 142
 55 Retrieve from water 142
 56 Retrieve over jump 143

6 READY FOR THE SHOOT **147**

APPENDIX A **155**

APPENDIX B **159**

Helen with Thorn watching the launched dummy.

I have been working for a long time with my team of Hungarian Vizslas on a variety of different shoots ranging from rough shooting on a one to one basis up to beating and picking up on large commercial shoots, where the numbers of birds can be in excess of 300 on a day.

My personal experience is only of shooting in the UK, but many of the same skills can be applied to various parts of the world, relating to their particular game and purpose bred dogs.

I have been classed as a revolutionist because I would never punish my dogs. I never found the need to shout at them, shake them around or yank on the lead. It was obvious these methods were not very successful as the dog would repeat the errors as soon as it was out of reach or out of sight.

I was aware that putting the dog on lead took away their hunting licence. By waiting until the dog had regained self control in that environment, I could then reward this regained control by slipping the lead and further hunting. This worked very effectively.

My dogs walk with me between the drives without being constantly nagged, and my dogs stay with me in the field. I knew I must be on the right track but there was also a big gap that needed to be filled. I wanted dogs that were able to think for themselves and adapt to the situations without constant direction from me. Along came positive rein-forcement, the clicker and Kay Laurence.

I instantly saw advantages in this method, that also built on the processes that I had already begun and filled in the missing pieces.

Through offered behaviours the dogs were encouraged to develop their own skill and think for themselves. The dogs learned quicker by the experience and non-directed learning and they seem to "understand" what is being asked. The level of communication between us increased and we developed a much better attitude to training. Suddenly I was able to capture the desire to learn and change completely from a reactive method to one of pro-action. Clicker training encouraged me to understand what I was doing based on the science of behaviour and I soon learned that infamous phrase 'what you click is what you get' and to make sure what I clicked for was what I wanted!

Hunting is a basic instinct, a genetically ingrained set of behaviours for the dogs. Their inherited skills have been honed over hundreds of generations and it is a wonderful experience, and honour, to work in partnership with them. The book looks at taking this natural skill, enhancing it and using it to enrich the partnership.

Good field work is a partnership between the dog and handler built on an understanding of the dog's ability to maintain self control and the handler's ability to understand this and the environment.

Writing Clicker Gundog has been both painful and enjoyable, but I hope one more dog and handler will go out to work in the field and demonstrate the joy of this training method.

Helen Phillips

sending Denie to "go on"

1 **Introduction**

We know from scientific evidence that the dog's origins lie with wolves and as such understand that hunting is one of their main instinctive drives. Refined hunting has been one of the key roles of the dogs we know today, evolving from partnerships with early man to the versatile individuals who live and work with us today.

Hounds developed excellent tracking abilities and characteristically sounding voice as they followed fur. Greyhounds, silent in comparison, were developed to use their excellent sight to follow quarry at high speeds, and bird dogs used to hunt with nose only. Although the use of dogs for hunting to obtain our food supply has almost been extinguished, the role has been transferred to a sport. This still includes most of the behavioural characteristics of the original hunting dogs: scent or sight capabilities and search and retrieve.

With the increase of food supplies from domesticated animals, hunting with dogs was taken up as sport and dogs were bred to hunt all types of quarry. Dogs hunted alongside birds of prey and quarry was captured with nets. Not only on land but also on water. In the sixteenth century following the invention of firearms hunting with nets and birds of prey gave way to the new sport of shooting. The dogs have since developed specialist skills and include the retrievers, spaniels, pointers, setters and the hunt point retrievers.

A VARIETY OF GUNDOGS

Different types of game and social influences have led to the evolution of a variety of gundogs. All can be employed at a shoot, but will have specialised tasks. There has been a preference for breeding dogs with a narrow range of highly specialised skills, and utilising more than one dog as part of the process.

This is a list of the predominant gundog varieties traditionally used in the UK:

SETTERS AND POINTERS

Specialised hunters that set or point on game birds. Mostly used in upland and moorland areas on heather and often worked in pairs. Not often used for beating or retrieving in the UK.

English Pointer   Gordon Setter   English Setter

Irish Setter   Irish Red and White Setter

Throughout the book the hunting skills for Hunt, Point, Retrieve (HPR) breeds can be applied to Setters and Pointer training in conjunction with appropriate terrain for these specialists.

SPANIELS OR FLUSHING DOGS

Used in close proximity, on all types of game. Not wide ranging, ideal beating dogs, excellent in woodland and driven shoots. Favoured as a rough shooting dog.

Cocker Spaniel	Clumber Spaniel	Springer Spaniel
Sussex Spaniel	Irish Water Spaniel	Field Spaniel

RETRIEVERS

Only used for picking up game, and will tirelessly work all day in that activity. Favoured where picking up from water is essential, and can be used for beating.

Golden Retriever	Labrador Retriever	Flatcoated Retriever
Curly Coated Retriever		

HUNT-POINT-RETRIEVE BREEDS (HPR)

All-round dogs that can carry out all tasks on the shoot. Often used on all types of game and as a rough shooting dog.

Weimeraners	Hungarian Vizslas	Italian Spinone
Large Munsterlander	German Pointers	Brittany Spaniel

FIELD ETIQUETTE

On a driven shoot **BEATERS** are organised by the **KEEPER** and are the group of people with or without dogs who work the ground in front of the guns moving the game up to points to be flushed. The **PICKERS UP** are the group of people with dogs who work behind the guns collecting up all shot game, they are also under the direction of the keeper. Ideally there should be one picker up for each gun.

A rough shoot is usually one gun and dogs, who will take opportunities as they arise and return home with only what they can carry.

At the end of the day all the game shot is food and as such should be treated with respect and every effort made to collect and store it appropriately.

GAME

Game is also often referred to as quarry and includes the following:

> Pheasant, partridge, grouse, ptarmigan, black game, common snipe, jacksnipe, woodcock, coot, moorhen, golden plover, curlew.
>
> Ducks and geese include gadwall, golden eye, pintail, pochard, shoveler, widgeon, tufted duck, mallard, teal, Canada, greylag and pink footed.
>
> Hares.
>
> Rabbits, woodpigeon and feral pigeons are not classed as game but pests although still shot and eaten throughout the season.

Some of the above can only be shot at certain times during the season. For example hares are subject to a closed season, and other game is restricted in places such as Scotland or Northern Ireland. You must make sure you are aware of the seasons before you set off rough shooting with your dog. On organised shoots the keeper will be versed in what is in season at that time and advise as such.

If you are thinking of entering any trials you would need to make yourself familiar with what is in season and what can be shot at that time. If you are thinking of working on a shoot you will also need to be familiar with what game is to be shot on the day, the keeper will let you know when you arrive.

No game can be shot on a Sunday or Christmas day this is against the law.

Sometimes shoots will engage in a mixed bag day that may well include other pests such as squirrels, beware of squirrels they are tenacious and will offer a nasty bite if not dead.

I have found that etiquette varies from shoot to shoot. It mainly depends on the keeper's perceptions and the type of game. Large commercial shoots are run as businesses where there can be over 10 guns shooting more than 200 in a day. These are run quite differently from a small personal syndicate shoot. On the large shoots the guns, transported around separately, often never see the beaters. The pickers up will be located behind the guns and traditionally only allowed to work at the direction of the keeper after the drive has finished. Some shoots in between the two will often allow the pickers up to work while the guns are shooting. This is often the best way as it insures all game is retrieved and despatched as early as possible. On smaller shoots the guns will often bring their own dogs and request to be allowed to retrieve their own birds. This can present problems if the dogs are not experienced; the gun is often more focused on the shooting than on what the dog is actually doing. The pickers up then need to have good eyes and mark all the game in case the gun misses some at the end of the drive.

THE LAW AND THE DOG

In general the laws that apply to dogs, owners and handlers still apply to the working dog in the field with some exceptions. These exceptions are as follows

▶ Dogs are not required to wear a collar bearing the identity tag when being used for shooting purposes this includes picking up.

▶ Dogs are not required to be on a lead when on a designated road whilst engaged in shooting purposes.

▶ Prior consent of all land owners must be obtained before dogs are sent to retrieve shot game otherwise they are deemed as trespassing.

▶ Handlers of dogs worrying livestock even whilst engaged in shooting purposes commit an offence.

The law also requires you to have a game licence if you are to be involved with the game in any way. This is especially important if you are expected to retrieve the game. The licence itself allows you to kill the game. This is important when the dog retrieves injured quarry, you are then responsible for instantly despatching it. The licence is not expensive, £6, and can be obtained from the Post Office.

You must also possess a game licence if you are picking up and be proficient in the despatch of wounded game. To do this humanely the use of a priest or commercially manufactured game dispatcher is recommended. A priest is a weighted heavy small truncheon like instrument designed to despatch game efficiently and be easy to carry.

Whether beating or picking up you should arrive in plenty of time and report to the keeper, shoot organiser or who ever is in charge of the beating line or pickers up. If you wish to take a young dog to a

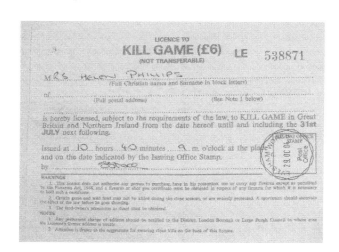

above: a game licence, to prevent you from prosecution as a poacher.

below: a priest

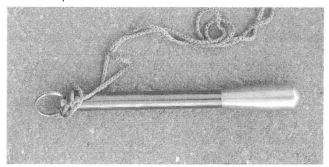

shoot to gain experience you should always ask permission of the keeper. Bitches in season are not allowed on shoots.

Remember if things get too much for you or your dog then withdraw, give your apologies to the keeper, and go back to training. It is much better to forego a day's shooting in the field than undo all the work you and your dog have already accomplished.

A GOOD FOUNDATION

The book looks at the behaviours required for developing any or all of the specialised skills. The standard of work is the same for this as for the competition field trials dogs, the difference being

- ▶ The amount of support you can give the dog in the field compared to the competition

- ▶ The quantity of cues you can give

- ▶ The increasing distance the dog has to work from you - in competition you must remain stationary for certain tasks but in the field you are more likely to be moving around with your dog (especially if you are picking up after a drive and looking for the runner or sweeping through after the drive to make sure no quarry is left behind)

- ▶ Duration of the behaviour. In the field the dog's control has to be maintained for greater periods than the competition dog, but the competition dog is required to turn it on for a perfect 10 minute display of all the elements

- ▶ More complex elements that are required, more re-direction for retrieve in competition than in the field

- ▶ The dog working for longer without reinforcement in the competition, reinforcement can be delivered at anytime while you are actually working in the field, this should be encouraged and the assumption the dog does the work because it loves it should be forgotten

Ultimately it is your responsibility to be intimately familiar with what is required from both your dog and yourself in either the field or competition. You should make several visits as an observer, and possibly video with permission, before you subject your dog to the environment. The field trial environment differs greatly from the working test environment and both are far from the thrill and excitement that can be experienced on a shoot.

HOW TO USE THE BOOK

The book is written in recipe form, each recipe is designed to develop one skill or criteria at a time. As the dog's experience grows it will naturally begin to make connections. At this point decide which behaviours are the weaker, which need further development and which can be developed alongside each other. By teaching them in this way you will also be able to break these connections down and rebuild should a particular part begin to deteriorate. This will also help you to make the decision at which point to take your dog into the shooting field.

The diagram below shows the order and balance of the areas of training which will help you understand which behaviours need to be in place before you teach other exercises. It is very important to make sure that the foundation behaviours are solidly in place before you move on.

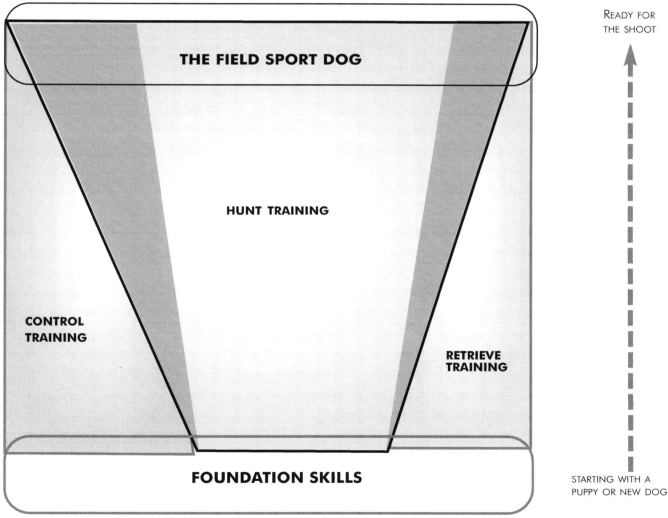

THE FIELD SPORT DOG

HUNT TRAINING

CONTROL TRAINING

RETRIEVE TRAINING

FOUNDATION SKILLS

READY FOR THE SHOOT

STARTING WITH A PUPPY OR NEW DOG

The foundation training underpins ALL the other training. If these foundations are not put in place correctly then the following exercises are very likely to break down. This applies in particular to establishing the soundness of Control before venturing into the environment of the shoot for the first time. So often new dogs come on the shoot and completely lose themselves in the hunting. The skills of hunting and control should be built gradually throughout the training and work well if developed alongside each other. Retrieve is a specialised skill that once developed can then be introduced with the hunting.

Taking a dog to a shoot to gain experience of the environment under managed conditions should not be confused with taking a dog to the shoot to work, either in the beating line or picking up, for the first time.

Unfortunately the sport still has a less than positive image based upon the way the dogs are handled and the misconception that unless you jump on your dog several times a day it will never have any control or be any good. You will encounter this and you will need to be prepared. I feel that the only way to make a change is for us to be there, train our dogs to a very high standard and show by example how things can be achieved differently. Wait for the questions to follow and then promote how to train this way.

Highlight the great parts of the day for yourself, for example, the one great retrieve or hunt and flush followed by kill. Store these and focus on them instead of the moments when things didn't quite go to plan.

I recall one of those moments when I need to strengthen myself against certain judgements or other methods encountered. I have a 7-year-old bitch whose skill in the field is excellent, her self control whilst working the game a pure pleasure to watch but through my early inability to communicate with her she never made the retrieve connection. Then came the clicker. Wow! Communication bridged. I was able to explain by making a plan, breaking down the behaviour to the smallest parts and micro shaping it. Suddenly retrieve became rewarding and last season we both achieved a first as a team, she hunted up, flushed a pheasant, I shot it and she retrieved it back. A perfect experience for me, one of those momories that stays with you for life.

USING THE BOOK

In order to get the best from this book I recommend that you understand the general clicker training principles that are covered in Foundation and Novice from the Clicker Trainers Series books from Learning About Dogs. You will also need to be familiar with Clicker Intermediate Training.

The main techniques that you will need to be confident in are:

1. Target with hand, mat or marker to acquire new behaviours and to be able to fade the target when on cue. This will be used within some of the foundation behaviours.

2. Free shape both complex behaviours like a good pick up for retrieve and behaviours that are physical movements such as the dog being able to swing its back end to re-position for the next retrieve.

3. Understand how to ensure that a behaviour only happens when cued and never unless cued and have the ability to teach this to the dog.

4. Train a behaviour to maintain strength and quality in a variety of different locations and increasingly difficult distractions

5. Have the ability to finish the behaviours to the highest standard required, either for the field or trial, and have attached the required cues. The spoken word is required to be kept to a minimal with the emphasis is on whistle or visual cue.

6. Combine the simple behaviours into the chains and merges, for example, retrieve, and marking the birds. Collecting together on a final cue.

7. Delay the reward, building the dog to be able to perform a number of behaviours for one reward and understanding what your dog actually perceives as rewarding.

I recommend that you begin with making a plan for training, this will need to take into account the time of year. Winter is the busy season for this sport and ideal opportunities for gathering experience for both the dog and you. Summer can be used to prepare and solidify your work, taking the dog through the processes of maintaining the required behaviours to a high standard and possibly using the working tests to develop both your skills. Consider the dog's seasonal fitness through the year.

Keep records of your training as it will be a long period of time from when you commenced training of the first skills to when you actually begin working your dog in all the elements, you will need to know what needs refreshing, what elements or skills were not ready and when to continue training as opposed to working in maintenance.

SELECTING THE PUPPY OR DOG FOR THE JOB

THE 'SENSITIVE' DOG

Dogs that make the best working partnerships are often those that are referred to as being 'sensitive'. This means mentally sensitive to all types of stimulus, such as noises, scents, sights, and from social interaction with other dogs, people, and activities.

This will later make them more skilled at being able to respond readily to the stimuli you wish to introduce, such as cue control, and also able to make selections between stimuli to react to and stimuli to ignore. You are looking for a good balance between the two but not a dog that is so sensitive it will react to everything.

Difficulties can arise with the puppies that have not been fortunate enough to have been reared in a rich environment. Those shut in a kennel, with little or no human contact or reared on puppy farms, are unable to socialise or experience new things at the critical developmental periods. These puppies will have difficulty dealing with new situations, lack the appropriate skills to cope with meeting other dogs and people, may also have depressed learning abilities.

LEARNING

Puppies are designed to learn different skills at different stages of their development. Learning is the process where the individual answers to changes in the environment with correspondingly changed and adapted behaviour. It is through this first contact with the outside world that puppies acquire vital knowledge that later will make a difference between life and death. Learning that water is wet, fire is hot, contact with hard items brings pain, what tastes good and what doesn't are all achieved through this contact. This mental knowledge has to be acquired by the pup itself and a young pup will throw itself into various unknown situations through lack of experience of the outcome. Curiosity will drive them forward but it will also be cured by their developing caution. A well-balanced relationship between these two factors will advance learning at the right pace.

EARLY ENVIRONMENTAL INFLUENCES

Early environmental effects on a puppy are called imprinting and will remain with it for the rest of its life. The puppies are imprinted to environmental stimuli that they will later on in life use to judge situations and take decisions. They are imprinted to members of the same species, food and everything that subsequently plays an important role in their struggle for survival.

Socialising is an activity best shared!

If puppies are not imprinted to people before they reach seven weeks old, they may never consider people as social or working partners. Imprinting is irreversible, and cannot be changed or deleted after it has taken place. Its effect may be reduced in relation to certain things like food and social needs.

This early learning process is the main reason for taking young puppies out into the environment you will be expecting them to work in, introducing the sound of gunshot, and encouraging retrieve as early as possible.

Selecting a puppy from the correct line is also just as important, as true bred hunting dogs that have worked successfully will also have developed a strong willingness to work in partnership and this is a very desirable characteristic to pass on. Alongside this you need to look for a breeder that is aware of the importance of developing the early learning in the puppy. The following is a brief guide to what can be done even as early as the neonatal stage to help prepare the dog for the job and what to be aware of and look out for when selecting a puppy or even a young dog for this type of work.

THE NEONATAL STAGE (BIRTH - 2 WEEKS)

During the neonatal stage the puppies are totally under the care of the bitch and rely on her for warmth, food, grooming, contact, comfort and safe retrieval. They are sensitive to touch, pain, temperature and taste while hearing, vision and temperature regulation is still under development. Their motor skills include the ability to suck, nuzzle and paddle but even at this early stage they have the ability to learn about righting themselves, comfort and conditions.

Mild stresses early in life help to fine tune the pup to respond in a more even and level manner later on rather than in the all or nothing way. Introducing the puppies at this early stage to some mild stress, such as a drop in temperature when changing the bedding or held in warm hands and gently rotated and rocked, can develop their mechanism to cope. If this early life is littered with human contact then this should stimulate beneficial development of their minds.

THE TRANSITIONAL STAGE (2-4 WEEKS)

The next stage in development is the transitional period when their senses begin to develop properly. Eyes and ears open and they respond to light and moving objects. Their temperature mechanism is improved and their pain response is similar to that of an adult, by three weeks they can stand and motor skills develop to walking. They are aware of their litter mates, bitch and human contact. They can taste and are able to nurse on their own. The bitches will often begin to regurgitate food and encourage them to eat for themselves.

Learning begins in earnest, they are aware of their environment, all their senses are being stimulated and the images encountered will influence the mind forever. They begin to explore and remember things; their memory has been awakened. They need play, contact with the bitch and their siblings for a while longer to develop to their maximum potential.

More physical and sensory development should be introduced at this stage; things should be changed within the environment,

▶ New scents these should include those the pup is going to encounter when working as an adult

▶ Lights   ▶ Different flooring   ▶ Obstacles

The pups should be:

▶ Handled, examined   ▶ Stroked   ▶ Massaged

▶ Gently groomed for stimulation

From four weeks on there should be no need to restrain noise, for developing gundogs introduction of loud noises, such as doors banging, buckets dropping, dinner bowls clattering, should begin. This is important to prepare the puppies for the sound of gunshot.

THE SOCIALISATION STAGE (4-16 WEEKS)

The next stage in their development is the socialisation period this begins when the puppy has developed all its communication faculties. They can see, hear, smell, touch and process the information. The puppies' brains are now ready for complex learning.

They develop the ability to play and learn about compromise. They should have as much interaction with each other and humans as possible. This introduces us into their lives, beyond just carers, and will help to build the relationship for the working partnership required later on.

This is the ideal time to get them out into the environment in which they are going to be expected to work, this can safely be done before the second lot of vaccinations as long as you have assessed the levels of risk involved,

- ▶ Short walks should be encouraged

- ▶ Retrieving anything and everything developed

- ▶ Obstacles introduced that will develop balance, climbing, confidence in being on different textures, perception of depth and

- ▶ Free range in a controlled environment arranged.

These should all be geared around play, learning is being introduced without the pups even being aware that it is happening.

TRIAL AND ERROR

The pups at this stage are beginning to learn by trial and error. As positive trainers we know how important this is to our training programme and confidence in using it needs to be developed and encouraged even at this early stage.

It is therefore very important that the puppies are not left unattended in the kennel for long periods. The puppies should be introduced to, as much differing stimuli available including that, which may be potentially fearful, like gunshot. See **INTRODUCING THE GUN** Recipe 1 *page 28* on how to achieve this.

If you are choosing a puppy or young dog to work in the field you will need to take into consideration not only the line but also the qualities and skill of the breeder in developing a sound base for you to continue to build on before you make your final choice.

CHOOSING CUES

Before you begin to attach cues to your behaviours think about how appropriate the cue will be for the behaviour. Make a list of the behaviours you will need and then plan the cues that you wish to attach before you start.

Using voice has long been discouraged in the shooting field as it is well known that the game can hear the quietest voices talking a long way off and their natural instinct is to move away, not always in the desired direction. This has encouraged the use of the whistle or body language to cue the dog for the behaviours required at distance. Verbal cues are still appropriate for the behaviours in close proximity for example the *sit* or the *give* on retrieve.

Unless you are very musical and a dab hand at blowing tunes on a whistle, its use is limited. As it is generally easier to begin with body language cues for both you and the dog, I have found it beneficial to save the whistle cues for the established behaviours, attaching temporary body language cues while building and working on the behaviour in question. Then working through the process of new cue old cue when changing to the final whistle.

The most common whistles are the 'Acme' 210, 210fi, 211, 211fi, 212. These are made out of a resilient plastic and can be easily replaced if lost. Choose the one that suits you the best; do not worry that it may be a common tone that lots of other handlers on the shoot may be using. It is the way that you blow the whistle that makes the cue.

The important aspect of this is to practice blowing the whistle, familiarise yourself with the chosen cue before you attach it to the behaviour. Make sure you remain consistent with this otherwise your dog will become confused and eventually the quality of the behaviour will deteriorate. I have found using the tip of my tongue on the end of the whistle helps separate the pips and maintain a crisp sharp sound, as it controls the airflow. The ones I prefer are without the pea.

Another choice of whistle is the silent type; the problem with this type of whistle is that if it is pitched too high you cannot hear it and will never know if you are repeatedly blowing the same cue. They can be set at a low level that can still be heard when blown so you can stay on the ball with your cue delivery and it is more likely that the dog will hear it at this level as well.

Another choice of whistle is the 'Acme thunderer' for the *'stop'*. this is quite a loud, referee whistle and is often used by the keepers to signal the end of the drive to the guns. This can be confusing if you choose to use it as your stop, you may inadvertently end the drive!

the Acme thunderer (left) and gundog whistle

More than one whistle to choose from can result in missing the moment for blowing the cue. I have found that one whistle adequately does all the jobs and I would recommend that you try out different types before you finally decide.

Once you have chosen a whistle it will be with you for that dog's life span, make sure you decide on one that you can live with and one that can easily be replaced should you lose it. This is very difficult with the hand carved bone types as each one has its own distinct tone and if lost it is not possible to replicate the tone and you may need to change the cues to a new whistle.

Body language can very effectively be used for the directional cues such as *right, left* or *back* as the dog will be looking at you when stopped on the whistle. Try to avoid waving your arms around like a helicopter. Be positive and consistent about your hand signals and the dog will have no trouble understanding them.

SOME EXAMPLES OF POSSIBLE WHISTLE CUES:

Long single blast for stop - peeeeeeeeeeeeeeeep.

Five short pips for recall - pip pip pip pip pip.

Two pips to turn on quartering - pip pip.

SOME EXAMPLES OF POSSIBLE BODY LANGUAGE CUES:

Right arm out horizontal from body = go left (remember the dog is looking at you so its their left).

Left arm out horizontal from body = go right.

Right arm held up straight and moving in a forward motion by your ear = go back.

Moving in a pattern from left to right across the field simulates the initial quartering and encourages a young inexperienced dog to follow and take note of changes in direction from you.

EQUIPMENT

It is important before you set off to consider what equipment may be beneficial to you, what you have access to and what you will have to adapt or develop in order to set up the scenarios for training closest to what is likely to happen when out in the field.

With clothing you need to consider neutral colours that will not scream out at the wildlife. I remember being at a shoot one year and waiting with some of the other beaters to set off when a new member to the team turned up. The weather was not good and it was raining, this new comer made his introductions and then went off to get 'kitted up'. When he rejoined us I thought the gamekeeper was going to have a heart attack then and there on the spot, he was wearing a bright fluorescent yellow jacket and over trousers apparently the only waterproof clothes he possessed! (Suitable for bear country!)

WELLINGTONS!

Following years of experience being out in all weathers and terrains I strongly recommend that the best piece of equipment for you to invest in is a top quality pair of Wellingtons. They come with either leather or neoprene lining. Side zips have come on leaps and bounds since first introduced, they make the task of taking the wellies off such a breeze now and they are perfectly waterproof.

You may gasp at the cost but once purchased they are worth every penny, providing warm dry feet, no blisters and support on your ankles, plus years of honourable service.

Eight years ago I asked, tongue in cheek, for such a pair as a birthday present, was lucky to receive them and have lived in them ever since. They are still as good as the day I had them. Before this I was replacing my ordinary ones on a seasonal basis so in the long term this has proved a very cost effective exercise.

You may prefer ordinary boots but again I would recommend that you invest in a top quality pair and look after them each season, oiling and keeping the leather water proof and supple. Saddle oil is great for this. The difficulty I always found with boots was the height up the leg and for me I was always the one having to cross the bog or stream that inevitably proved to be deeper than the boots height.

Boots will require gaiters in the winter. Gaiters are leg protectors that come over the top of the boots but below the knee, again good quality is a must otherwise they are not water proof and ineffective. Boots are ideal for spring and summer training but for me 'wellies' are best.

If you are on a budget my advice would be to get the wellies as first choice as they will service you well throughout the whole year.

LEGGINGS

These come in several different types: the all-in-ones that pull on like trousers, the ones that have separate legs that attach to a belt. Make sure your choice are strong, tough, waterproof and long enough to cover the top of your 'wellies'. These will then provide protection against brambles, undergrowth and keep you dry when the rain is running off your coat and down your legs. Good materials to look for are the oiled wax or a very strong nylon.

My choice after trying out both types is the pull on ones as they provide a waterproof seat that can be very beneficial; you can sit down anywhere remaining dry at the same time. Some beaters buses/trailers double up as the dog kennel at lunchtime the result being very wet dogs enjoying the pleasure of snoozing on the seats followed by wet beaters bums for the afternoon session.

BIRDS AS TEACHING AIDS

It is very difficult if you do not have ready access to real game birds or to set up scenarios to build strength and durability into the required behaviours. I have covered some ideas here to help you overcome this stepping-stone. The keeping of birds as teaching aids should not be looked on lightly, their care and management should always be the priority.

BOB WHITE QUAIL

Bob White Quail are not native to our country, originating in the states. For keeping Bob white quail some space and some skill in bird management is required along with some knowledge of the laws relating to the release of non-native birds into the country. You

Top: Cock Pheasant
Centre: Grey Partridge
Bottom: Hare

will need to research and learn about their management before attempting to keep and use them as a training aid. Quail are not game as defined by the laws of this country, as such cannot be shot although they can be farmed as 'domestic' fowl and served at the table.

They do however make excellent teachers for the dogs in that they generally take off and fly straight up instead of great distances. This means that they can be placed out and used effectively to teach the dogs to hunt by scent. They must not be used to shoot over the dogs.

They soon settle as a group or 'bevy' and are easily recalled to a pen if you keep the majority back only releasing the few you need to train with that day. When released they return to the safety of shelter and reliable food source. You will need to build funnels on the side of the pen that allow the birds to re-enter but not escape.

They are readily available in this country, suppliers can be easily located on the Web.

The laws relating to the release of non-native birds into the wild have not been greatly tested, this testing has fallen, mainly to the keepers of exotic birds like parrots. These birds are often found free flying and the general belief is that if the birds are tame returning each day to shelter and food they are in effect not released into the wild. Following the recent out breaks of bird flu DEFRA have begun to keep records of poultry and game keepers with 50 birds or more, at the moment this is not law but may well change in the near future. If you decide to keep these quail as an aid I suggest you keep up to date with any relevant changes in the law relating to this.

PIGEONS

Pigeons are a different story as they are native to this country. For centuries pigeons have been happily kept in lofts at the end of the urban garden. I do not intend to go into depth here about how to keep pigeons or any other birds that you could use to help train your dog for the sport.

There are plenty of excellent books out there that will help you with bird management.

PARTRIDGE

Partridge can be kept in a similar way to the quail but only the young will return to the pen. As they mature they will disappear off to find territory of their own and will need replacing each season.

RABBITS

Rabbits can also be kept in a pen if you have enough space, again you will need to research the best way to manage and care for them. I am not referring to the domestic pet rabbit but to the wild type. The ideal size for flushing dogs like spaniels is two beats wide and a good distance in length to achieve some good hunting ground. For the HPR's it is much more difficult to create a large enough pen to recreate the beat but one the size for the flushing dogs is excellent to use when working through the Control Recipes.

HARES

Hares are very territorial. Go out onto your training ground and spend some time locating them. Plan training sessions in these areas with the likelihood that the hare will offer itself up nicely as a teaching aid. In some parts of the country hares are almost extinct, dedication as a trainer will have to come to the fore in these situations and you will have to go and find some.

RETRIEVE ARTICLES

These can be as varied as you like, the more variety you introduce the dog to the more skilled they become at generalisation, exactly what they will be expected to do with variety of game.

The conventional retrieve articles are the green dummies that can be purchased from any good field sport supplier. These also come in a variety of colours including orange, khaki and white. I have always found the ordinary green ones to adequately do the job. The majority can now be located without difficulty on the web.

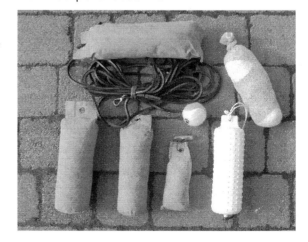

I would recommend the essentials

- ▶ Puppy dummy

- ▶ 1lb green dummy

- ▶ 1lb dummy covered with rabbit fur

- ▶ Old sock stuffed with more old socks

- ▶ Tennis balls or similar

- ▶ Squeaky toy

- ▶ Soft toy - for the traditionalists amongst you these now come looking like ducks, geese and pheasants! Personally I just use my good old teddy bear off the bed

- ▶ A water dummy that will float, these now come looking like ducks I believe, mine is just a plain white tube filled with air attached to a long piece of string

- ▶ A bundle of wings or two wings that can be attached to one of your dummies

- ▶ Cold game which can be stored effectively in the freezer, this should remain intact

- ▶ Rabbit fur

Other retrieve articles that may be useful if the budget allows

- ▶ 3lb green dummy

- ▶ 6lb hare dummy these now come fur covered which is very useful and weighted to teach the dog to balance the pick up

THE DUMMY LAUNCHER AND DUMMY

This is a piece of equipment designed to be fired using blanks and launches a dummy into the air whilst making a noise 'similar' to shot. A word of caution here, I have a very old launcher that is user friendly, easy to handle and which hardly gives any kick when fired. The second newer launcher I obtained was lethal nearly taking off my husband's thumb when he fired it. I suggest you wear gloves and take care when using for the first time. I believe that a certain specialist supplier now produces a launcher that is fitted with a stock similar to a shotgun, I have no experience of this type yet but it may well be worth a try.

You will also need a tool to remove the blank from the launcher after firing. A 6" nail or a small flat screwdriver from a Christmas cracker is perfectly adequate. The launcher comes with a variety of dummies. I prefer the soft foam or canvas type.

▶ Blank firing pistol, used for stimulus control, 'similar' sound to gunshot.

▶ Bolting Rabbit

The bolting rabbit is a green canvas dummy attached to a long length of strong elastic. When the elastic is pulled taught and released the dummy is released across the ground at great speed and force. Make sure you, or your dog, are not in the way, it can give a nasty bash from the dummy or whip burn from the elastic. Make sure you have fixed the end securely before stretching the elastic taught, I do know of someone who sustained injury when the end came loose and whipped back. The dogs can also become very aware of the noise on release so this becomes the cue to the dummy flying past and very quickly they are able to ignore it. I have one, but have never used it.

▶ Live pigeon case with remote release which folds flat, a useful tool for containing the birds when teaching the hunt recipes.

SCENT

Natural scent is now readily available in dropper bottles for all different types of birds. It can be used to scent your dummies. Remember how strong the dog's nose is and only use sparingly. A tiny, tiny amount can be used to introduce the puppies to the scent before they are old enough to go out and about.

LEADS AND COLLARS

This is what I train and work my dogs with and refer to during the different recipes. The quality of this equipment is a priority. The different leads, collars and harnesses should be well made with strong reinforced stitching on the joins, any clasps or clips should also be securely fixed, glued and stitched is best.

▶ 6ft standard webbing lead with an elastic handle -for loose lead walking

▶ Standard webbing collar correct size for your dog with good strong release clip -for loose lead walking

▶ Rope slip lead, avoid nylon material as these are stiff and uncomfortable to hold. This is for use in the field when your dog has the skill to walk on a loose lead

▶ Standard webbing harness correct size for your dog, for use with the long line *(picture right)*

▶ A long 30ft or 10m line, light weight but strong, I use a thin rope used for climbing which is easy to manage, very light but extremely strong. You will need to adapt a means of fixing a clip on the end or become adept at tying a good knot. If buying climbing rope ask the supplier to fix a clip to the end for you. Kite string is also an alternative. Fix the rope or string to a stout stick that you can then wind or unwind the slack round as required. You can grip it with one hand and tuck it under your arm to provide a more secure hold.

Other useful equipment

▶ A game bag to put your dummies, game and any other equipment in.

▶ A game carrier for when you are in the field and working with your dog picking up.

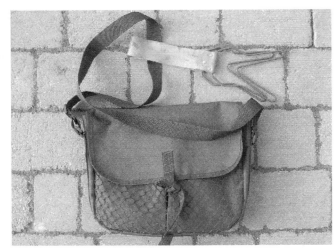

2 Foundation Skills

TO BE A DOG

As clicker trainers we learn how the dogs are influenced by their environment and how quickly some behaviours are associated with particular places. It is also important to allow dogs to be dogs and enjoying free running, sniffing and hunting just for the pure pleasure of it. An opportunity to check out the special scents, the rabbit holes when and how they want to. They will quickly memorise these locations and be naturally pulled towards them. If I beat a particular shoot several times in a week, the dogs will begin to go straight to the places where the game is rather than work at hunting right from the start. If left to their own devices, and having already satisfied the need of hunger, the dogs would probably just enjoy their territory for what it is. In order to be able to do this you will need to establish a place that you can take your dog to, where they can free run and enjoy the environment, and there should be no stimulus control or association with the working environment. You should not use this special free time place to train your dog, find somewhere else to do this and keep them separate.

By using the dog's ability to memorise different environments you can have two grounds - the first for free time, down time and de-stressing, and the second for training, work and under stimulus control. By not mixing the two expectations the dogs can enjoy their free time without making the error of relaxed hunting on the shooting day.

THE SOCIAL DOG

Working your dog in the field can be a very sociable experience. In general beaters and pickers-up are a friendly lot and are there for an enjoyable day out with their dogs doing what they were bred to do. You will meet a vast variety of people from all walks of life with a range of different interests. Your dog will also be expected to meet a great variety of different people and dogs of all shapes and sizes.

If you are beating you will likely be expected to travel in the beaters 'bus'. This can vary from quad bikes, open trailers, covered tractor-trailers to old Bedford vans. I am sure there are many more variations on this. When travelling on this transport you will be in very close proximity to each other and so will the dogs. Temperament has always been one of the main selection qualities in gundogs but even so it is still important to make sure your dog has developed the skill needed to cope with this situation. It is a very different thing being out in open space working alongside other dogs to being sat with noses touching.

Kemble dislikes this close proximity; she is a dog that has an area of her own space around her and takes umbrage with any who enter it. She deals with this by taking up residence under the seat out of the way. She is quite content to be there and requires no further management.

Take time to familiarise your dog with being in close proximity to other people and dogs right from the beginning. I always take my young dogs to town where I use the shoppers desire for non-interaction to help familiarise them and make assessments of their sociability.

If the need then arises I will look for opportunities to click and reward for proximity of dogs and people.

FITNESS TO DO THE JOB

When working in the field your dog will require a sound level of fitness, as will you to some degree. You will be expected to work all day, arriving at the shoot, ready to begin, at around 9 am. You can expect to finish at dusk. On partridge days the amount of distance covered may be twice that as a pheasant day, and the terrain you will be walking will also vary greatly from set aside (unploughed land) to heavily ploughed fields (hard work) or woodland (tricky footing with lots of obstacles). If your dog is picking up on the big commercial shoots they will be expected to collect birds all day. This is quite a feat in its own right without all the hunting that may have to go with it.

You will need to plan the feeding routine of the dog and be aware of the symptoms of torsion and bloat that some breeds can suffer. If fed before a day's work keep meals small and allow at least 12 hours for digestion before hard work.

I have created a safe and calm environment in the back of the car where the dogs can relax and they would prefer to be in the back of the car than left at home in their beds. My husband and I travel around 2 hours with the dogs to a shoot in Wales; they will sleep on the journey to and from the shoot and I can feed them in the car before the journey home. Conditioning the car to become a second kennel or home for the dog.

Your dog will work in all weathers, the shoot doesn't pack up just because it's raining or snowing. Plan for this and get your dog used to being out in all weather. My first Vizsla hated the rain and always managed to find somewhere warm and sheltered to sit when she was picking up, often under a hedge or in the lip of a ditch. Her favourite place was under the bottom of my coat tucked tight up against my leg. Taking care of your dogs well-being right from the start means they will have a much longer working life. The twelve year old can still do a full day's work. Prepare for the wet make sure you dry your dogs before putting them to rest either at lunchtime or for the journey home. Make sure they are warm when they stop work. If they get cold after they have been working hard they will become stiff, this can easily lead to torn muscles and even joint problems later in life. There are lots of good quality coats on the market that can be used to keep them warm on the journey home. A warm supple dog will be able to perform much better than a cold stiff one.

Take some water with you, this may sound a little strange but I have been partridge shooting in the early part of the season when it has been hot and sunny; all the usual places to get water were bone dry, the dogs were working hard in the heat and susceptible to dehydration and heat exhaustion.

HEAT EXHAUSTION:

(a) First signs of heat exhaustion are incessant panting and obvious distress.

(b) The dog should be cooled immediately by sponging or hosing down with cold water, ensure the head is drenched.

(c) A wet towel frequently changed will help cool the dog down and in a hot environment may help to prevent heat exhaustion.

FIRST AID KIT:

Always carry a first aid kit in the car along with the telephone number of your vet in case of emergencies. Some ideas;

Absorbent cotton wool

Cling film (useful for an emergency bandage will keep wounds clean until arrival at the vets)

Adhesive and gauze bandages (2" and 4" may be useful)

Gauze swabs	Sterile wraps
Cotton buds	Scissors, sharp pointed
Thermometer	Tweezers
Forceps, medium sized, blunt points	Plastic syringe 20 ml
Eye drops	Ear cleaning drops
Antiseptic ointment	Antiseptic wash
Antiseptic spray	

Learn how to put on simple bandages such as a tail or ear bandage. These extremities on the dog are often the first part to be caught up in brambles or the like and they will bleed profusely as the blood vessels are very close to the surface. This can be very useful in protecting the interior of your car while you transport your dog home or to the vet if need be for treatment.

AN EMERGENCY MUZZLE

The ability to put on an emergency muzzle may also be useful especially if the dog has been caught up in something. Even the best mannered dogs when in pain can reflexively bite. This bite is not directed at you but at the area or obstruction causing the pain. You are just in the way.

Use gauze bandage, a tie, torn cotton sheet or other soft material as the muzzle. Make a loop large enough to slip over the dog's muzzle. Quickly slip this over the dog's muzzle and tighten. Do not tie in a knot. Cross under the muzzle and wrap behind the dog's ears. Tie in a secure bow. Restraining a short muzzled or very small dog will be easier by wrapping in a towel or something similar.

REGULAR CHECKS

Check your dog over at the end of each day to make sure there are no thorns or injuries. Dogs are extremely resilient and will keep working even when injured and some injuries will not bleed enough to notice immediately. Allow your dog some down time at the end of the day where they can walk about and gradually reduce the build up of lactic acid in the muscles.

At the end of the season your dog will have a very high level of fitness, this should be brought down to a more sustainable level for the out of season months by gradually decreasing the amount of exercise. Before the following season gradually build your dog's fitness by increasing the amount of exercise to about an hour a day, developing the muscles on different terrains. Work through the jumps to build strength back into this skill. Take the dog swimming if they enjoy it, which is an excellent way to build muscle, strength and flexibility with minimum risk.

Introduce your dog to as much variety in terrain, crops, woodlands, open fields, hedgerows, walls, fences, marshland etc., as this will build flexibility into their knowledge and help them adapt to different situations. Look at each environment and give the dog experience of negotiating different fences - going under as well as over, jumping fallen logs, into rivers, streams, lakes, ditches and ponds. Walk off the beaten track and look for learning opportunities.

When Kemble was a young puppy I thought I had introduced her to pretty much every type of ground and crop that we were likely to meet when shooting in our part of the countryside. But I had not planned for a field full of marrows. She was convinced they were a field of living creatures at first sight. I had to withdraw from the drive and go back to teaching her how to manage herself through such "beasties".

INTRODUCTION TO THE GUN

With my own dogs I do this as early as possible, for the young puppies this takes place during the socialisation period. I do not tip toe around in the pen where the puppies live, doors are banged and dishes clattered when put to the floor. This forms part of the everyday routines. I am also fortunate to live on a farm where often pigeon shooting takes place so the puppies can hear this on a regular basis but at a distance that will not cause alarm. I also have three generations of working dogs that I can use to help with the introduction to the gun.

This must take place in an environment that your dog finds secure, is familiar with and associates with some pleasure. I do not believe that the dog should be controlled or managed at the time, they should be free to make any physical move they feel necessary. Your job is to ensure that the environment is safe for them. A long safety line may be applicable but not used to manage the dog in any way other than to prevent flight over a great distance.

RECIPE: 1

INTRODUCTION TO THE SOUND OF THE GUN

You do not need to have your own shotgun to do this, a starting pistol or dummy launcher will do. There is a difference in the noise but it is irrelevant in the initial stages of introduction. You can develop this when taking your dog to experience the environment in which it is going to be expected to work in.

PUPPIES

- ▶ The pups go out into a specific field with all the older dogs, enjoy their company, share the scents and become comfortable with the environment.

- ▶ Once familiar, look for the signs that they are feeling confident before proceeding.

- ▶ Enlist the help of (a husband) a gun and ask them to begin firing a shot from behind the hedge in another field.

  On hearing the noise the pups look to the older dogs for indication on how they should react. The older dogs inevitably don't react other than an acknowledged look with some excitement, the puppies pick up on this and it is turned into a routine event.

▶ Gradually reduce the distance of the gun from the pups until the shot can be fired whilst walking along with the puppies. This experience is then stored within the puppies' 'toolbox' of essential skills and gradually built on as their experience develops.

OLDER DOGS

I would use a similar set up to introduce an older dog the sound of shot. If you only have one dog then enlist the help of some of the members of your local shoot who work their dogs. Establish an environment that is safe and familiar to your dog, invite along the rest of the group plus someone with a gun, and go through the process as with a puppy, making sure the first shot is fired at a distance, observe your dog if you see any signs of hazard avoidance, flight or distress developing then stop, withdraw and go back a couple of stages until the dog is confident again.

It should be a pleasurable and enjoyable experience for your dog, that will make an essential link: loud noise = pleasure scents, hunting etc.

Avoid introducing any stimulus control, such as sit, or down at the beginning. This can be developed alongside and brought together later when your dog is confident with the noise.

Difficulties arise if the pup has experiences of loud noises used as inhibitors to unwanted behaviours: for example the rolled up newspaper bashed on the table makes a very loud noise linked with the shock, and a young dog may well make the wrong connection. The damage is done; any loud noise is then associated with a bad experience. If the dog is older and subjected to the noise of shot in close proximity, without any prior preparation this may cause great distress that will remain with them for life.

Gun shyness is a nervous reaction to loud noise, I understand that some dogs do have more sensitive hearing than others and this may contribute to it, but I firmly believe that if the experience is essentially a pleasurable one in the first instance, the noise attaches itself to this pleasure and even the most sensitive hearing becomes accustomed to it.

This is a general life skill that can be developed without using the clicker. If you do use the clicker you will need to have exceptional timing and be sure of what you want to click for. This is an experience that is made up of many different skills, some of which will be emotional for example excitement, self control, awareness, a little uncertainty and anxiety at the beginning. A miss timed click may attach to the wrong aspect of the learning.

Keep this exercise separate from the other behaviours in the beginning until your dog has begun to gain experience. The last thing you want is to associate any anxiety with a skill such as the drop or stop.

THE RECALL

This will be a lifelong project and the minute you become complacent about the behaviour and its solidity is the time the dog will be in the wrong drive flushing the birds or run in to retrieve. Yes, I do carry treats with me and yes, the dogs are rewarded for prompt response in as many situations as possible. This keeps the recall strong, sometimes it can be rewarded with the immediate return to hunting, other times for example if the drive has stopped, it is rewarded with the food. Prevention takes a few moments every day, a cure may take the rest of the season or prematurely end the dog's career.

Many times whilst out in the field I have seen dogs failing to respond to the recall. Sometimes it is lack of preparation, where the stimulus of the environment has outweighed the stimulus of the control cue, dog and handler have moved on too fast, but the majority of the time it is insufficient reinforcement of a classically conditioned behaviour. The real skill of this is not establishing the behaviour but keeping and maintaining its quality.

Dogs hunt because they love it, it is not instinctive to break off hunting and return to the handler. The value of reinforcement must be redressed and the conditioned response to cue maintained. You will associate the return to you as an integral part of the hunt. The science of learning has to be applied and the rules abided by.

The recall is an indication of the relationship between you and the dog, it needs to be strongly established before moving onto the more specialised recipes and definitely in place before you consider taking part in your first organised shoot day.

The ideal scenario is to begin with the dog as young as possible when their desire to be with you for security and protection is still present. As clicker trainers we look for hundreds of opportunities to reinforce the return: acknowledgement, approval, toys, games, food, continuation of activity. The conditioning process has begun and the partnership is in the process of being built. This behaviour will only be taken into situations of high level stimulation (distraction and environmental), when the stimulus (cue) has become a conditioned response (a reaction rather than a considered "shall I or shan't I?")

With puppies and younger dogs the majority of this can be achieved without the use of a lead but there may be situations or scenarios especially with the older dog who is just beginning, where you may not be the higher value reward at that time and for safety reasons the use of a long line and harness is recommended.

This critical exercise is one of the hardest to achieve and may take many months to develop. Make sure you have planned your rewards before every interaction. With fast growing youngsters food will likely outweigh all others, for the older dog you will have to dig deep into your tool kit and use rewards such as the continuation of hunting, tracking, scenting or some free rabbit pooh. All of this is building towards the idea that you are the access to, and a key part of, the hunting process and not ancillary to it.

It is easy to transfer the pleasure received from one activity to another activity. Very often the less pleasurable activity can gain value by using the high pleasure activity as a reward. For example, if your dog loves to race after the ball when you throw it, show the dog a ball and ask for sit. The moment he begins to sit, click and throw the ball. The race after the ball becomes the reward for the sit. Once the dog consistently sits for a ball, begin to use the reward ball-fetch to teach "sit and stay", by moving from an instant of sitting before throwing the ball to minutes before throwing the ball.

This will build a very strong reward association for your dog; if you always make racing after the ball (hunting) contingent upon controlled sitting (in preparation for retrieve), your dog will look forward to sitting with as much pleasure as hunting, because he will begin to anticipate hunting as a good reason to sit.

RECIPE: 2

RECALL FOR PUPPIES

I introduce the puppies to the recall whistle cue. I do this in the litter as soon as the pups' hearing has developed, repeating it as often as possible. This becomes classically conditioned and if regularly reinforced and maintained can be developed into the strong recall used later in the field and through life. Decide on your whistle cue and practice it before beginning.

1. Take some food and scatter around the floor as the pup is eating make your whistle cue

2. Repeat this many times during the day and consistently for about a week

3. Include some calm approval, such as stroking the dog, scratching ears and talking softly to them as they are close by, again make your whistle cue. Create the idea that being close to you and having contact with you is a great place to be.

4. Change the sequence around and whistle the cue; as the puppy arrives scatter some food around your feet.

5. Increase the criteria, whistling the puppy from one location to another always reinforcing the prompt arrival.

6. Change to feeding from the hand. You are beginning to introduce your hand as a target for the dog to locate to.

7. A high value reward such as food will need to be offered on every occasion for at least the first 100 times, may be more.

This whistle cue is never followed by something unrewarding like returning to the kennel or lead on. The reinforcement will always come first followed by the end of the walk, time for bed etc. This is continued throughout the dog's life and develops into the conditioned recall for use in the field.

This works just as effectively with older dogs and is a good place to begin to redress the balance if being close to you is not more rewarding than being out.

RECIPE: 3

TARGET HAND

This is very useful for bringing the dog in close to you when you need that extra control: the beating line has stopped and you need to wait for new instructions or maybe the birds are very skittish and need to settle before the drive continues. I use it too develop the sit in front for the retrieve and it is a useful behaviour for measuring the stimulus levels for the dog in the control exercises.

1. Begin by placing a piece of food between your middle fingers, offer the back of your hand to the dog and as their nose touches your hand to sniff the food click and feed from hand, remove the lure after three repetitions.

2. Mimic the placing of the food between your fingers and offer the back of your hand to the dog, click for the touch, and reward from your reserve.

3. Change to offering the back of your hand, keep it close and click for the nose touch, when there is no hesitation introduce your 'touch' cue just before you offer the hand.

4. Begin to feed to the floor, consolidate the behaviour and then increase criteria to throwing the food away.

5. Build this into a strong behaviour with some distance, then take it outside.

6. Introduce your whistle cue; click as the dog responds, offer target to locate the hand signal and reward.

7. This needs to be conditioned to the point of being an automatic response, no choice, this can then begin to be introduced to the hunting and retrieve exercises and these skills can then be used as high value reinforcement for prompt response.

8. Begin to introduce your changes of direction to this so that the dog begins to develop the skill of keeping one eye on you. This is important from the hunting perspective they need to know where or what the group is doing in case one of the group has hit on a good scent and this needs to be followed up. Introduce a 'this way' cue. This develops well with **THE CATCH UP GAME** Recipe 30 *page 96.*

9. Observe your dog and when they are aware of you in relation to what they are doing, change direction, call *'this way'* and keep going. Click the dog as they go past, and reward with the continuing hunt. If they do not respond then find something of vast interest at ground level, making noise of exclamation. With some observation practise or even just watching where your dogs head out to, you can memories where the game birds have been roosting and investigate this. When they arrive click, and the reward will be the successful find. *"Hey I can hunt as well you know".* Dogs always fall for this!

10. Mix together the two criteria of changing direction on *this way* and coming in close to your *touch* cue. Keep this unpredictable so the dog never knows which will happen.

11. Introduce an interim behaviour as well; ask the dog to complete a behaviour such as sit, or wait, before being sent off again. Use this to have contact with the dog in a calm way, talking softly and stroking. This will help with preventing the dog from running in to you and immediately heading off again, it will also begin to introduce some self control and give you chance to assess the dog's reaction to the increasing levels of stimuli. My dogs all love to have their ears rubbed and squeezed this has a calming effect on them; I introduce this at this point.

12. If hesitation in response to your cue begins to creep in drop back down a criteria and build the behaviour back up. Decrease the distance or level of stimulus from the environment or distraction.

Keep this unpredictable. Recall in itself is not a single behaviour and it requires a number of skills or strategies from us to keep it reliable. Combine this with the control exercises and with distance work as this will help the dog keep its ears open. Incorporate it into the working walks.

The development of this will need to progress slowly, introducing criteria one step at a time and consolidating it before moving on. Location changes, levels of distraction and distance are all just increments in criteria. Lots of repetition of this skill will keep it fresh and instill in the dog's mind that returning to you is not going to end the hunt but may involve other, just as rewarding, activities such as a 'go find' or a 'fetch'.

If necessary for safety reasons introduce the use of the long line when you move to a higher level of distraction or stimulation or to a new environment.

RECIPE: 4

THE ELASTIC RECALL

When teaching the recall to the puppies or young dogs I often equate it to the principle of 'yo-yoing'. Yo-yoing them to and fro, they respond to the whistle, give a hand touch and then be sent off again immediately. This can in itself be a very good game as well as teaching vital skills. Older dogs will love to do it as well. It is also very good for building speed into the recall.

You will be teaching the dog the skill to

▶ Return to you with speed

▶ Return to you with purpose

1. Begin with teaching the target hand and gradually throw the food further and further away. Find food that is easy to throw and visible. This will encourage the race back to you for the next piece. Some distance will be required to do this.

2. As the dog turns back and looks at you for the next 'cue' hold out your target hand, give your 'touch' cue, click the dog for the touch and throw the food away.

3. Move yourself to the middle of the yo-yo zone. Change the timing of your click to select for speed as the dog approaches, turn away from the dog and throw the food, this should encourage the dog to race past you.

4. Keep yo-yoing the dog to and fro. Always selectively click for speed and the direction towards you, using the food to keep this momentum up. If you feed on arrival the dog will begin to slow down in anticipation of the stop and you will not be developing this purposeful run at speed.

5. Once the speed is established re-introduce your whistle cue for recall, deliver it just before the dog turns to return, this will likely be as they are eating the food.

6. Again build up your level of distractions and change your locations. If throwing the food outside is not an option, then seek the help of someone (or two people) to act as a food station(s) who will deliver the food on the click. As the skill builds in strength this person moves further away from you to increase the distance.

You have now taught the dog the skill of running towards you, the next step is to teach them how and where to arrive. Later, this will be used to develop the sit in front for the delivery on retrieve.

RECIPE: 5

THE SIT IN FRONT

Again this behaviour should be taught separately to the fast recall so that you maintain the quality of both. Teaching them together will cause a loss of the speed on the return or the dog crashing into you instead of a sit in front. For the sit in front the distance you are looking for is close enough for you to be able to reach out and take the game without stepping forward or leaning over the dog. Too close and the dog will be shoving the game in your midriff which is not too clothes friendly, especially if the game has been hit hard.

The skills you will be teaching the dog are

▶ To locate a position relative to you

▶ To sit in this position

▶ And to re-adjust themselves if required on arrival

Begin by teaching your dog the skill to side step so that they can then straighten themselves up on cue from you. Teach both directions, as you will need them to be able to locate from all approaches, as everything is variable in this sport. This is also a fun skill to teach and is light relief from some of the more complex skills that the dog will need later. Teach it using your free shaping skill. Consider two cues for use on each direction.

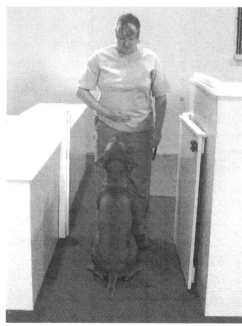

Using natural barriers to encourage a straight sit in front

1. Begin by free shaping the dog to stand on a stool or low box. Make sure the stool isn't too high; the dog should be able to locate, balance and be comfortable on the stool before moving on.

2. Begin to develop one sideways movement at a time, encourage the dog to approach from the side, place the reward at the side of the stool and click for the rear foot movement as the dog straightens up to look or face you.

3. Then place the food in a position so the dog has to make the biggest side stepping movement to face you, click when the dog reaches the position straight in front of you.

4. Attach your cues; these can be verbal to the different directions.

teaching the dog to angle straight in front

5. Then stand up behind the stool, with your shoulders straight and your hands in your final cue position, either in front or straight by your side. Click the dog for moving into the 'straight' position in front of you after standing on the stool.

6. Build flexibility and strength into this by moving around the stool and getting the dog to counter balance and straighten up in front of you *(pic left)*. Attach a verbal cue to this final position.

The next stage is to teach the dog the location and to use your shoulders as the guide for "being straight".

Observe how your dog sits, if they sit backwards (where the front feet move towards the back feet on sitting) then you will find it easier to teach them the front sit (where the back feet walk towards the front feet) on another cue.

If they sit backwards they will naturally move away from you as they sit, which increases the distance you have to reach to take the retrieve. Use your hand target and teach the dog to sit whilst maintaining the contact.

1. Carefully teach your dog to come into the front of you using your hand target. Draw the target hand in centrally and click on contact, throw the food directly behind the dog so that they can relocate again back to the target.

2. As the dog begins to locate easily onto this target begin to throw the food out in different directions, always click for contact on the target. Remember one criteria at a time so that means from one direction at a time. Your dog will probably be more fluent from one direction than the other build up flexibility in this using your sidestepping behaviour separately.

3. You are building a chain, so use your individual cues to develop this and build accurately. You have your target 'touch', your sidestep 'left' or 'right' depending on what is needed and your cue for 'forward' sit. Click on arrival at target, feed and then set the dog up for repetition by tossing a piece of food away. Hard work deserves just reward.

4. Your final cue for this chain will be the way you stand, so make sure you have rehearsed this before you start. As soon as your dog is fluent and has begun to anticipate the chain of behaviours before cue, begin to drop off your verbal cues. Your dog will then cue off your body language. Keep the shoulders straight!

5. Follow the recipes in Retrieve Training, Chapter 5, page 119 to bring it together.

RECIPE: 6

POSITIONING THE DOG FOR DIRECTED RETRIEVE OR SETTING OFF AGAIN

If you decide to do any competition or enter working tests to gain experience for your dog you will need to set up your dog for the mark or the second retrieve. This looks much more professional if you can cue the dog to make the movement itself. The dog can either go around the back of you and locate to your side or swing into the position from the front. This can be developed from your side stepping behaviour already taught from the previous recipes.

For teaching the swing from the front use your stool again:

1. Begin by positioning the dog in front of you as before then move yourself into the location at the side of the dog. This will begin to encourage the idea in the dog's mind of a new location at your side.

2. Then using your hands and body as well as your swing cue move the dog from the front position to the side position, initially click for the movement, and then change the timing of the click to the final location.

3. Then remove the stool and develop first from the stand then from the sit in front. Then build with your sit and mark in the location from the retrieve chapter.

For teaching the dog to go round behind you:

1. Begin first by teaching the dog to follow a short target stick following the recipes in the Foundation and Novice books from the Clicker Trainers Series by Kay Laurence. Whilst standing still take the target stick around behind you, changing hands half way and bring the dog to the location by your side. Maintain the target stick vertical just above the dog's nose this will keep them quite close.

2. Click during the movement and feed in location. Once fluent introduce your *finish* cue and again build with the sit and mark from the retrieve chapter.

You can then build using your cues for the dog to move to the left or right to accurately set them up in the sit and mark ready to be sent off. This is especially useful for blind retrieves when you want the dog to go straight out from you in the right direction.

RECIPE: 7

CHIN TO HAND TARGET

This is very useful for helping the dog to locate to hand for delivery of the retrieve and links in well with Retrieve Training, Chapter 5 *page 119*. Often young dogs will find it hard to hold a retrieve and lift their heads up. By using the hand to chin target you will have a solid behaviour to begin with that the dog will be able to instantly recognise and locate to.

Begin teaching this following the recipe in the Foundation Book P67, for teaching *Sleepy* by free shaping. This is another good way to build fun into your teaching and develop a working partnership. This position is very comforting to the dog; often puppies will lie with their head and neck across each other soaking up the warmth. My older dogs are often found sleeping with their heads and necks across each other in front of the fire in a more refined version of the puppy pile.

1. From teaching *Sleepy*, introduce a target mat to place under the head. Something that is flat but not the same as the target for the re-direction work later in this chapter. A different texture, shape and size something like a beer mat or soft coaster.

2. Place this mat on the floor between your dog's front feet and cue sleepy begin to develop the targeted behaviour.

3. Place the mat on to a low surface and cue sleepy and gradually build up the height until the dog can do it sitting, then standing. Finally fade the mat replacing with the palm of your hand, introduce your new cue 'chin'.

THE SKILL OF SWIMMING

The majority of gundogs are natural swimmers and love nothing better than doing it for pure pleasure. There is a skill to it and experience alongside confidence is also required. Some dogs find the paddling action difficult to master at first, causing them to lift out the water at the front end whilst the rear end sinks, lots of splashing but no movement. This is one of those skills where practice does make perfect.

Introduce a puppy or young dog to water as early as possible. I give my puppies bowls to play and splash about in from around 6 weeks on. The last litter of puppies found the new pond in the garden and introduced themselves to swimming at a very early age whilst watching the older dogs splash around and chase each other.

Begin by finding a pond or lake with still or very slow moving water. I would not recommend using the river for the first lessons as the currents can be very strong, the water may be still on the surface but moving at great speed underneath. Watch out for the blue green algae that appears early in the year this can be very harmful and sometimes cause death, it is toxic to us as well.

Find somewhere that the dog can enter and exit the water easily via a gentle slope. Be prepared to enter the water with your dog. This may be all they need to build the confidence to take the first step. Taking a favourite toy may also be helpful if they are reluctant.

If your dog is a little hesitant then spend time playing with them in the shallows and gradually let them make their own choice to enter further, click for the decisions and reward with chase for a toy or food if appropriate to the bank.

The dog will need to keep their body flat on the surface of the water and develop a paddling action with their feet. If your dog is having difficulty then help them by supporting under their belly slightly raising the back end until they are flat, click for this position, and gradually reduce your involvement. Reward with a chase of a toy to the shore, or being allowed to leave the water.

Take your time and do not rush this. My first Vizsla, as a young dog, fell in the river, the shock of this was so great she never entered water again. She walked around puddles, in case they were deeper than they appeared, the trauma can have a lasting effect. Make sure your dog is confident in entering the water before introducing the retrieve.

Using the retrieve to teach the swimming may work with some dogs but the shock of entering the water may develop avoidance of both the retrieve and swimming in others.

Once established and your dog is confident attach your swimming cue, this will be used to cue your dog to enter the water when building the chain with retrieve.

RECIPE 8:

SHAKING ON CUE

When leaving the water the dog will naturally wish to shake, this is normally no problem unless they are carrying game. The enthusiasm and force that is put into shaking results in the game having the appearance of a rag doll. It can also encourage the dog to grip tighter than normal so as not to let go, or the force throws the game from the dog's mouth. Capture the behaviour and attach a cue.

1. Set up the situation where the dog can leave the water easily and you can be in close proximity.

2. As soon as the dog shakes, click, reward appropriately. This can be with verbal encouragement from you, continued shaking, or food if your dog will accept this, or even back for more swimming.

3. Set up scenarios at home, douse your dog with the hosepipe and capture the shake from this. Dogs will shake even if a small amount of water is on the top of their head, they do not need the full body shower.

4. Anticipate when the dog is going to begin the behaviour and attach a verbal cue to it. Build on this until the behaviour only happens when cued.

This can then be introduced when your dog is retrieving from water, the dog will deliver the retrieve to you on leaving the water and wait to be cued to shake. See **RETRIEVE FROM WATER** Recipe 55 *page 142.*

THE SKILL OF JUMPING

Before you teach your dog the skill of jumping you will need to be sure that they have finished growing completely and all their bones are fully mature and set. Growing bones have soft growth plates which the impact of jumping can damage. If you teach a dog too early to jump you risk damaging their bones for life. There is plenty of time to develop this skill when the dog is ready.

Introduce puppies and young dogs to the idea of obstacles by enriching their environment with things that they can climb on, balance on and crawl through. All this alongside experience in different terrain like mud, set aside, crops etc., will begin to put in place the foundation that you can then build on when the dog is old enough to start.

Some dogs are natural jumpers and will grasp any new challenge with relish, others are more cautious and will take time to build confidence. Whichever dog you have it is important to teach both the skill of jumping safely to reduce the long term impact this can have on their bodies. The natural jumpers will throw themselves into the task but may not focus on the jump resulting in a poor take off or landing.

If you will be travelling to different parts of the country to work your dog, then find out what the obstacles are likely to be in these places. Familiarising your dog to them in your jump training. I remember once someone told me they had travelled a long way to go shooting with their dog on ground that was broken with stonewalls instead of fences. The dog was at a complete loss as these walls created a barrier that they had never encountered before. To us they appear an easier option to climb but from the dog's point of view were a solid wall that prevented any insight in to what lay on the other side.

Barbed wire fences are a major concern to your dog's welfare. Some are only low level and the dog can be taught to jump these safely. In some areas there are deer fences these are much higher and often have three strands of wire pulled tight across the top. It is a difficult dilemma. The size of your dog will dictate the maximum height they can jump safely and the fence will cue the dog to jump. Finally you need to take into consideration that jumping while carrying something heavy will also reduce the height that the dog can safely jump. Have a go yourself drape something heavy around your neck and experience what impact this has on your ability to jump.

Here are some points to consider before beginning your jump training

▶ The fence is a barrier that is only jumped when cued by you this will mean that you will need to be up with the dog to check the fence before sending your dog over it. This can be difficult in some working situations.

▶ Teach your dog to only jump a certain height with confidence, building inhibition of anything higher. This will need great skill and experience on your dog's part and intensive proofing on yours.

▶ Teach your dog to confidently jump the maximum height they are physically capable of managing. Build this with experience and decision making on your dogs part when out working. A clicker trained dog is very good at making decisions and solving puzzles.

My young dog, Thorn, can easily scale a five bar gate with confidence now. When he was younger he cleared the gate on the way to a retrieve but having picked the bird, a heavy old cock pheasant, made the decision on the return that the jump was too great so he put the bird down jumped the gate, put his head through, picked up the bird completing the retrieve. Not the most practical of scenarios, on this occasion the bird was stone dead but it could quite easily have run off when he put it down, but putting his safety first was a far more important skilled decision. Even now if he is unsure of his ability to successfully make the return jump with the game he will look for an alternative way back. This may involve taking a long diversion but if dog and retrieve return safely this has to be the priority. This skill builds with experience and is a good skill to develop when you are working your dog in the field.

▶ In competition these days because of health and safety issues and dogs sustaining injuries from barbed wire, the judges will or should check a fence before asking you to send your dog. If you have taught your dog to jump with confidence at their maximum height then this will be a breeze for them.

▶ You can purchase from good field sport equipment stores a 'fence protector' this is designed to fit in your pocket and can be fixed to the top of barbed wire fences protecting you and your dog as you get over them. The majority of us use the plastic flags attached to the end of our sticks.

RECIPE: 9

JUMPING

You will need to make a jump that can be adjusted easily to gradually increase the height, some suggestions are

▶ Two big cones and plastic pole

▶ Some bricks with holes in that can be stacked to different heights and pole

▶ The poles used for horse fences that can easily be pushed into the ground, suitable length of plastic pipe with string threaded through that then hooks on to the poles. These are good as they go up higher than the cones.

1. Begin by placing out the two posts to your jump, set your dog up so they are running confidently between them. You can use the food thrown ahead of them or two points of reinforcement, such as small tables that you can put pots of food under.

The dog needs to be focused on looking ahead and not at you. If they are watching you then when you introduce the jump they will begin to jump twisted. This may cause injuries later on. Move slowly behind the dog letting the dog reach the reinforcement point ahead of you.

2. Once travelling confidently through the posts, introduce your pole; place it on the floor between the two posts. Click your dog for stepping over it and feed from the table.

3. Gradually increase by a small distance at a time until the dog is jumping confidently, clicking for the take off, when this jump is of consistent quality introduce your *over* cue. The majority of the time a poor landing occurs is because of poor take off or the dog has twisted in mid air to look at you. By being consistent with the take off and making sure you are not in the dog's eyeline as it jumps the landings should take care of themselves.

4. If your dog begins to stumble at a particular height increment, stop and drop back a level make sure this is confident before moving up again. It may be that your dog has reached its maximum height. Jumping fitness will be developed with practice, and the height may increase over the next few months.

5. Increase the distance of the tables from the jump as the height increases to allow your dog enough run up.

6. Build strength and flexibility into the jumping by introducing the dog to as many different types as possible out in the field.

Some dogs are 'natural' climbers and can scale wire fences and hedges several feet taller than themselves. This skill appears to be genetic to the dog. I had a German Short Haired Pointer many years ago and he developed the skill of being able to use the wire to aid his climbing. Instead of actually jumping the fence he climbed it and pushed himself off the top. Learning by experience, I assume, where to safely put his feet on the wire at the top. Spaniels seem to be very good at this. Where we go shooting in Wales, the Spaniels are brought up on ground surrounded by sheep fences and seem to naturally develop this way of getting over.

When we went to see our second Vizsla Denie, her dam was in a kennel in the garden that had six foot fencing with a wire roof on top. The explanation for the roof was that the bitch was an excellent climber and the fence alone could not keep her in. Denie it appeared later had inherited this skill along with the ability to climb hedges in her younger days. None of Denie's generations since have shown this skill. If it appears it can be enhanced through clicker training but a difficult skill to develop from scratch. This skill was encouraged in the European HPR's and there are some wonderful pictures in the old books of Vizslas climbing trees for a retrieve.

You can find further variations on jump training in the Clicker Agility book.

DISTANCE WORK

Before teaching your dog the skill to drop, stop and redirection you need to have developed their confidence in working at a distance from you. If you have always rewarded for close proximity your dog may well find working away as a loss of reward and feel punished by this. These behaviours are crucial to your hunting and retrieve chains so you need to avoid contaminating them right from the start. The behaviours should not be used to develop the skill of working at a distance from you as any anxiety or stress that the dog feels by being away from you will transfer to the behaviour.

RECIPE: 10

WORKING AT DISTANCE

Throw food to your dog when it is at a distance so that they begin to understand that being out there can be rewarding and is a Good Place to be. Use this throwing action just as the dog turns to look at you with that questioning look on their face 'what now?' and launch the food behind. This will begin to teach the dog to pay attention whilst out there, as you never know what may happen next.

If your dog keeps creeping towards you and is finding it very difficult to adapt to staying away then introduce a barrier or manage the dog with a line. Put the dog behind a fence and throw the food over to them as before. Or hitch the dog up and throw the food as before and gradually increase the distance making sure that you take time with each step to build up the dog's confidence. Do not begin teaching the drop or stop until your dog is confident at being away from you without a barrier or line.

Develop two skills into this, the first where the dog remains static and you move, keep the dog in position with the food and you gradually move away, and secondly where you keep the dog moving and you remain static.

Introduce some behaviours to teach the dog the skill of listening while at distance, simple things like sit, down, jump will do and vary them. Initially the dog will try to come back to where they associate these behaviours should be happening. Use your skill of food throwing and your developing stay out there signal or use the barrier or hitch up technique. Ten paces away should be enough to begin. Use food that throws well, hot dog sausage travels well if cut into chunks instead of slices, as does kibble.

Taking time with this will also help with your recall training, by teaching the dog the skill to listen while at a distance will encourage them to pay attention while away from you - something worth while may happen. As dogs begin to mature or as distance increases they sometimes develop selective deafness. These games will help you over come this.

RECIPE: 11

THE DROP

This behaviour will replace the link in the hunting chain at the flush/catch. In the natural hunting chain this behaviour will normally be one of a launch into the air after the bird or a launch out in front after the ground game. Both include clearance from the ground. Teaching the sit at this point is half way to allowing the dog to launch themselves in the air. In order to sit, they lift their head up which tempts the follow through after the bird. By teaching the drop it becomes a contrary behaviour to their natural response and will be much easier for them to maintain self control.

In order to achieve this you will need to think about exactly what is required and when it will be required. The majority of the time the dog will be facing away from you, moving and in order to take the impetus out of the launch, the dog's head will need to drop first. The perfect behaviour is the hinged drop, with head first into the down, remaining in the lion position for ease of setting off again. The best way to achieve this is to set up a scenario and capture it.

Before teaching this take some food and lure the dog into the position and exercise the dog in the movement developing muscle memory. You know yourself how stiff you feel if you exercise using muscles in a new way. Avoid this with your dog, the last thing you want to do is to associate pain with such an important behaviour that will be the end point of your hunting chain. Build suppleness and flexibility into the movement before you begin capturing it. Just use the food to lure between the stand and the drop. No need to click, as this is just exercise and the dog's brain and nose will only be engaged with the food.

Find somewhere that has a long run, like a hall way, and something that you can throw food under that will encourage the dog to drop head first to get at it, such as a side board or cupboard or a home made sandwich board *(see picture right)*.

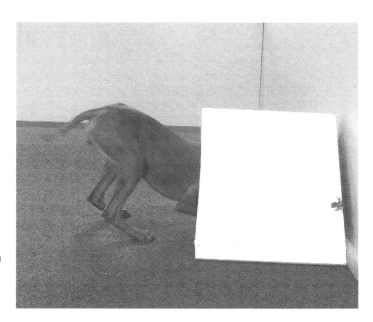

This will need to be deep enough that the dog has to drop down to get far enough under to capture the food. A wall at the back will also help, if your furniture is free standing the dog will likely run round or jump over to capture the food. Use food such as kibble that will roll fast under the cupboard and encourage the dog to chase after it, exactly what they will be doing on the flush, this will then teach the dog the skill to engage in the behaviour whilst on the move.

1. Begin close to the dog and the furniture. Let the dog see you throw the food underneath, use an underarm throwing action and click the dog for any attempt to get underneath to retrieve the kibble.

2. Continue with this until the dog is comfortable dropping their head and diving underneath.

3. Gradually move yourself further away so the dog has a run up to the capture and make sure you withdraw your hand signal from the throw as soon as possible, you want to avoid this becoming a cue. Throw from behind the dog; they will soon learn to watch where the kibble is going rather than where it is coming from.

4. Gradually change the timing of the click to when the dog drops completely, head first followed by rear end.

5. Build strength, reliability and then attach your verbal *drop* cue.

6. Begin to move the behaviour from the barrier.

7. You will need to build this behaviour on the verbal cue so that it is fluent and reliable outside before you begin to use it to develop further with the recipes in the hunting chapter. The quality of the behaviour will determine the final quality and reliability of your drop to flush. You will be using the flush of the bird to become the new cue.

8. You will also need to build strength into this behaviour at a distance. Make sure when you fade the barrier that you keep the dog working at a distance from you, use the food, throw it randomly to keep the dog moving.

   Initially, when fading the barrier the behaviour will deteriorate slightly. Use your click to rebuild it, click for the initial anticipation and then build on this. Also take the time to build some duration into the drop, move up to the dog and kneel or sit beside them taking time to gently fuss them, rub their ears, making sure they remain in the lion position, talk calmly and remain calm yourself. This is a behaviour that you wish to take any excitement from.

   The act itself of flushing the bird will generate more than enough excitement to increase heart rate. Introduce an interim behaviour to take the dog out of the drop, such as hand touch, stand, recall and vary this so the dog does not begin to anticipate the next move. If you always follow with continued hunting or retrieve you will be building a longer chain and the dog may well find these behaviours more reinforcing. The quality of your drop will deteriorate as will the duration of it.

Separate the training of this behaviour and your recall. You will want a good, speedy return and if you begin to introduce the drop this will deteriorate. It will introduce an element of confusion in the dog as the drop behaviour is unlikely to be required on a recall and the dog will be torn between wanting to respond to the stimulus of the cue and being conditioned to return to you.

This is a fun way to capture this behaviour for both you and your dog. Enjoy it.

RECIPE: 12

THE STOP

This behaviour is best captured in the circumstances that you require it to happen. Develop good throwing skills. Do not set up a chase element but accurately throw the food to an area behind the dog. Throw against a wall, aiming for the skirting board and using food that is going to land and stay put, like the chicken pieces.

Avoid encouraging the dog to go off 'hunting' for the food. Your objective is to keep the dog at the wall using your food. The first behaviour you will need to capture in the dog is the skill of stopping still; this will then be merged with the sit to complete the stop. Attach a hand signal to the behaviour first which will be quickly recognised from your throwing action. You will need to have already taught the dog the behaviour of sit on

Step 1 - above, giving the dog a reason to stop, and stay "out there".
Step 2 - right , adding the sit.

verbal cue. For this the backward sit is appropriate, as it will take some of the natural impetus out of the forward movement. Teach this as a separate skill from the recall and the redirection, if you teach it together it will create conflict internally in the dog as they will want to come to you in response to the initial cue but you ask them to do totally the opposite. It will take a very experienced dog to be able to cope with this internal conflict. It is unlikely that you will recall the dog to you and then redirect on the way. In my experience you are more likely to want to redirect as the dog is heading away on a hunt for a retrieve, but in order to do this the dog will need to be able to stop, sit and look at you.

You will be teaching the dog the skills

- ▶ To stop still on the move

- ▶ To adopt the sit position

- ▶ To maintain the position at distance

- ▶ To watch you

1. Begin by being quite close and in front of your dog, take a handful of food and use the over arm throwing action to get your dog's attention. When they are watching throw the food behind them and allow them to collect it. You may have to do this a few times until the dog gets the idea that the food is going to be thrown over their head. Use some of the games in **WORKING AT A DISTANCE**, Recipe 10 *page 44*, before you begin.

2. As they turn back towards you be ready with your raised arm and move your hand as if to throw as the dog stops still to look, click and throw the food behind again. Keep repeating this and remember you are clicking as the dog becomes still, it doesn't matter that they will be standing at this stage. You are teaching them the skill of stopping. This hand signal will be your cue for not to return.

3. Create an imaginary line in front of the dog or use a marker to help you. Your objective is to keep the dog behind the marker using your hand signal of the throw and by feeding behind the dog. Gradually throw your food further behind the dog, they will naturally be drawn to return towards you, keep the distance.

4. Gradually develop the behaviour of stopping, and decide on a good hand signal, gradually reduce the movement in the signal until the dog stops on the upraised hand. Strengthen this behaviour.

5. Then when the dog is still introduce your verbal cue for 'sit', click for the stop still, cue sit and feed behind the dog for the sit.

6. Change the timing of the click, use your hand signal to cue the dog to stop still, cue the *sit* that will click the stop, then click the sit and feed behind.

7. Repeat until the dog begins to anticipate the sit on the hand signal and fade away your verbal 'sit' cue. The stop may deteriorate slightly at this stage but once you have the sit rebuild the quick response back up.

8. Use the food to maintain the distance from you. Take your time here and build confidence in your dog at working at a distance before changing the criteria.

9. Then begin using your food to get the dog moving round, your skill is to use the food to keep the dog away from you, whilst building strength into the behaviour.

10. When the behaviour is of top quality, only then introduce your whistle 'stop' cue.

Once you have established this behaviour you will need to proof it as much as you can. Take each change you make as an individual criteria jump and build generalisation and flexibility into the behaviour gradually. You will need to change the environment one step at a time and make sure that you maintain the quality before you move on. If you are losing the prompt stop, or the sit is deteriorating then go back, the behaviour is not strong enough to continue.

The next step will be to build some duration into the behaviour and introduce using an interim cue to end. You need to take the anticipation of moving off instantly to collect the food. Return to the dog and feed in position, following the steps for building duration in **SIT STAY,** Recipe 24 *page 77.* Use a cue to end and reset up again. You will also be delivering the dog a double whammy in not only a food reward but reward by you returning to them.

DIRECTION

Before you begin to teach these skills to your dog shape them to target a mat with their two front feet following the recipe in the Foundation Book, *page 75.*

Teach each direction individually to begin with. You will need two identical target mats plus a third later on for 'back'. I would suggest something like a flat plastic marker spot that can be thrown easily. It is large enough for the dog to locate with two feet and is a bright colour that will show up in long grass when close.

You will need to decide on appropriate cues for these behaviours, the traditional ones are the outstretched arm signals to either right or left, but if you are really good with the whistle this would make excellent cues, but remember the dog will be facing you so it will be their left and right not yours! Avoid verbal cues, as the dog is likely to be some distance from you, and as already discussed in the introduction, shouting is to be discouraged. These behaviours will sequence on from your *stop*, be careful not to train together as they will gradually become a chain that will reduce your quality in the duration on the stop, the dog will begin to anticipate a further hunt, and this is very likely to be more reinforcing than what can be offered in the duration.

RECIPE: 13

LEFT AND RIGHT

1. Having already targeted the dog's feet to the mat begin by throwing the mat all around building the dog's ability to be able to locate it from any direction in relation to you. Click the dog for prompt arrival on the mat and feed back in front of you. Make sure the dog can see the mat at this stage. Begin to established a 'mat' cue. Build this slowly maintaining the dog's confidence and speed. This mat target needs to be strong before moving on.

2. Introduce a sit before the mat is thrown. Cue the dog to go to the mat. You are building the dog's skill in being able to move from the sit, the adopted position for the stop, at speed to locate the mat. Click for prompt arrival and feed in front of you.

3. Change to placing the mat in a specific place to either the right or left of you. The mat should be close by to begin with and situated so the dog has to turn to either the left or the right to locate on it. Pick the side your dog is most confident in going to initially. Sit the dog in front of you making sure they can see the mat, cue 'mat' and click for the prompt arrival, feed back in front of you. Continue to build this until there is no hesitation, then gradually change the mat cue to your visual hand signal click for the arrival on the mat and feed in front of you. This yo-yoing will keep the speed in the behaviour.

4. Gradually move yourself away from the mat so that the dog begins by going out 4 feet but comes back 6. Build up to a good distance where the dog can still see the mat from the set off point in front of you.

5. Carry out the same steps for teaching the opposite direction, build both up to the same quality and fluency and introduce your cue for that direction.

6. Both behaviours need to be reliably on cue before progressing further. Introduce both mats about 15 feet apart; begin by sending the dog on cue to either the left or right, click for prompt arrival and feedback with you.

7. Add distractions slowly, take your time in building your dogs confidence.

8. Do not fade the mat yet. The dog will need to have confidence in going out in the direction sent and that the mat will be there to locate even if they can not see it when they set off initially before fading takes place.

9. Gradually begin to move yourself so that you are closer to one mat than the other, send the dog to the furthest, click on arrival and feed appropriately, move yourself closer to the other marker. Repeat. You are building the dogs skill in being able to move from one mat to the other on cue.

10. As your dog increases in confidence you can begin to gradually move yourself away until you form a triangle with the two mats.

11. Gradually increase the distance of the mats to 30 feet plus, fading them in long grass or stubble where they cannot be seen initially by the dog when setting off. Slowly build in distractions.

RECIPE: 14

BACK

Teach this skill before or after 'left' and 'right' as a completely separate exercise, making sure that the other two behaviours are on cue before you start. It will take a very confident and adaptable dog to deal with learning all three directions at the same time.

1. If you decide to teach this skill first then begin with steps one and two from the previous Recipe 13.

2. Change to placing the mat in a specific place in front of you. The mat should be close by to begin with, and situated so the dog has to turn back to locate on it. Sit the dog in front of you making sure they can see the mat, cue 'mat' and click for the prompt arrival, feed back in front of you. Continue to build this until there is no hesitation, and then gradually change the mat cue to your visual hand signal 'back' click for the arrival on the mat and feed in front of you. This yo-yoing will keep the speed in the behaviour. Make sure your hand signal for this is a moving signal and not similar to the one you used for the 'stop'.

3. Gradually move yourself away from the mat so that the dog begins by going out 4 feet but comes back 6. Build up to a good distance where the dog can still see the mat from the set off point in front of you.

4. Add distractions slowly, take your time in building your dog's confidence.

5. Increase the distance from the mat by moving away from it until you reach the point where the dog can no longer see the mat, 30 feet or more again.

6. Then begin gradually to move yourself away from the dog, so the dog learns the skill to go from any point between you and the mat.

7. Build in your distractions.

Eventually you will be sending your dog out in either direction blind on the promise that they will be locating their mat. This will be interrupted by the scent of game, or more likely a retrieve, which will cue the chains and reinforce the re-direction. This will need to be repaired to maintain the distance as you are using the longer distance to acquire the shorter in the field and too much high value reinforcement such as the retrieve or scent for the hunt on the shorter distances will discourage the dog from ranging.

You will need to build in the skill of going over obstacles and out of sight where the land slopes away from you or there is a hedge or fence in the way. Introduce the jump following the **RETRIEVE OVER JUMP** Recipe 56, *page 143* but without the retrieve. Build this with the mat remembering you are teaching the skill of going out in a particular direction. Be careful not to train too much in one field as your dog will learn to pattern very quickly and begin to follow imaginary lines from previous send outs making it difficult for them to change direction and follow a new line.

3 Control Training

DRIVE

The word 'drive' is often referred to in dog training, but there seems to be little consistency in its definition and is also confused with 'modes'. The dictionary definition of drive includes words like *"urge, impel, energy for getting things done"* along with all the others that apply to the movement of machinery or the propulsion of a vehicle. It can be used to describe the way an activity is carried out: *"he worked with drive"*, which implies hunting with purpose and propulsion, or the mode the dog was in whilst it was working: *"in hunting drive"*. Drive has different meanings to different people and is often used to explain or excuse behaviour.

In simple terms, 3 different types of drive are useful to understand:

- ▶ Prey drive

- ▶ Pack (social) drive

- ▶ Defence drive

Each of these is made up of a number of elements that equate to getting the job done. For example: prey drive is made up of the elements of chase, scenting, capturing, killing, etc., basically the hunting chain that is referred to in the chapter on hunting. These elements are instinctive and innate to our dogs.

Pack drive is made up of the elements of social interaction: touching, grooming, approval, attachment, awareness of the group. We use this drive interspersed with prey drive to develop the control and working partnership.

The defence drive is made up of protectiveness, guarding, fighting and one we hopefully will not have much dealing with for the purpose of a field sport dog.

A dog would naturally swap back and forth between these drives depending on what was the priority at the time. When "in drive" or under the influence of a particular drive, its actions and response can be shaped by that drive. The resulting behaviours can be different. A wolf out patrolling territory, marking boundaries, is likely to be in defence drive. If he comes across likely prey, but ignores them and continues, then the lack of hunger has not switched the wolf to prey drive. It remains in defence drive. On another occasion if the wolf were hungry the sight of the prey would trigger an immediate swap into the prey drive and this would then take priority over all else.

Field sport dogs have a high desire to work in the prey drive, especially those from well bred stock with the right sort of opportunities for development and learning. On this basis we build our training. It is questionable that ALL gundogs, whatever their breeding will have sufficient or suitable genetic inheritance to make a working dog.

PACK HUNTING

Co-operative pack hunting is also a part of the field sport dog make up. From the outset cooperation resulted in survival, and dogs most likely to work well as part of a pack (team) became the contributors to the future of the breeds. Continuation of this natural selection has bred finely tuned dogs that are able to listen, respond, exercise their own judgement, work with their own initiative and have the ability to quickly swap from drive to drive, or even work with both drives simultaneously.

These abilities may not show themselves initially but it can be developed through learning. It is likely that this dog only needs low levels of stimuli to swap it to prey drive but needs higher levels to swap to pack drive. It is therefore easy for this dog to be in prey drive which excludes everything else but much more difficult for it to be aware of your presence and much longer for it to actually respond to you. Each dog will be different in this.

Kemble always put the needs of the pack before anything else, she requires minimum stimuli to respond to the group, always appears to have one eye on the group even when hunting and has made an excellent dam. Because of this she would appear the ideal dog to train. To swap her to prey drive was much more difficult needing very high stimulation before she would engage. I developed a stimulus in the form of a cue to trigger this switch for her. My young bitch Rioja is the opposite, she is very much easier to swap into prey drive and would be stimulated to hunt even in the garden to the exclusion of everything else. With her I have to lower the level of the prey drive stimulation to be able swap her into pack drive in order to develop the co-ordinated pack hunting that I need.

PUNISHMENT

As the levels of arousal rise in the prey drive it becomes increasingly more difficult for the dog to respond to any other stimuli and to swap back to pack drive. When this happens the dog is not ignoring the handler, or exhibiting 'dominant' behaviour, or having difficulty understanding or listening. When working in the field the dog is multi tasking to a very high degree and aural cues are only likely to have a fraction of the impact of all the other stimuli. It is simply that they have had to give themselves over to the environmental stimuli that triggered the hunt in the first place, and they are "driven" to respond to the exclusion of all else, including us.

During this heightened state of arousal the adrenalin levels will be high, which dulls the dog's response to pain. As the dog is not able to respond to the pain, either physically or mentally, the amount of punishment delivered has to escalate. I always equate this to experiences in my previous job as a police constable; dealing with drug users was always far more difficult than non-users, especially when they wanted to fight. The levels of the drugs within their system heightened their arousal and adrenalin levels so much that they appeared to have super human strength and any pain was inconsequential, this always resulted in an escalation in the required levels of restraint needed to get the job done.

In order for the punishment to be effective the dog has to drop back from the prey mode into pack drive or if the punishment is great enough even into defence mode a place we definitely do not wish to put our dogs.

In order for the physical punishment to be effective it has to outweigh the compulsion of the prey drive and for it to be high enough to achieve this, it will swap the dog straight into the defence drive. This results in an association between the behaviour and pain that is likely to develop some form of avoidance, fear or aggression.

This has a major impact on our cues, as cues are only another form of stimuli. If the dog fails to respond to the stimulus/cue and the result may lead to punishment, the cue will begin to signal the opportunity for the dog to take avoidance. This means the cues we have been using for these behaviours become both a threat and a promise combined. If they are part of a chain and were being used in association with a specific behaviour, all the behaviours in the chain begin to break down, deteriorate and even possibly extinguish. A dog that once showed keen eagerness to do the job will begin to be reluctant or even show signs of stress and anxiety. Karen Pryor refers to this as 'poisoning the cue'.

Stress is a healthy reaction and serves self-preservation and prepares the dog for dealing with extreme situations. When the dog senses danger, stress prepares it for fight or flight (defence drive). The perception of prey stresses the predator so that it concentrates its energy ready for the moment of chase. But high levels of stress can become a problem when it causes pathological responses, for example, disease or abnormal behaviour. These responses usually occur if the dog has remained under stress for too long or too often. Learning itself is a stressful process, as the individual must deal with new impulses and confront the unknown.

We aim for learning that is stress free, or low level, in order not to increase it further to a point where learning becomes impossible and fear or avoidance behaviour result.

EXTINCTION

Clicker trained dogs are used to working things out, exploring options, and trying different behaviours until they find the right one. This is reinforced by us and all the other things that were offered begin to fade. When they reach the point of offering only the one behaviour to the exclusion of all else we begin to increase the criteria and the process begins again. This extinguishing is part and parcel of the learning programme; it encourages the dog to learn in a natural way: by trial and error.

Extinction is not punishment. Punishment simply decreases the likelihood of the behaviour being repeated. With extinction, the unwanted behaviours get no reinforcement and fade away.

Let's look at the dog that chases the rabbit.

The fleeing rabbit has triggered the dog into prey drive and the chase commences. The traditional way to deal with this is to set off hell for leather after the dog and catch it before it catches the rabbit. I have two difficulties with this, firstly, my sprinting is no match for Linford Christie and secondly, my stamina for maintaining the chase out of Roger Bannister's league.

If I chase after them waving my arms about screaming and shouting (with very little chance of catching them or the rabbit) then I am very likely perceived by the dog as encouraging the hunt and reinforcing the behaviour of chasing. If this ends in a successful catch, it will add heavy reinforcement to the behaviour of chasing.

If the situation allows it and you can 'intercept' your dog, by successfully putting yourself between the dog and the rabbit, this sudden appearance will likely stop the dog in its tracks. But, you will have to rugby tackle your dog to stop it from continuing. If your dog is sensitive to your interaction and even if the punishment is used correctly it may well have lasting side effects, including fear and aggression. The dog has dropped straight from prey drive into defence and you may have introduced avoidance into your hunting chain.

If you need to extinguish a behaviour, make sure you :

> have removed ANY possibility of an associating reward

> make the reinforcement for the preceding behaviour much stronger

> introduce a control behaviour that has a high reinforcement history

> are in control of the environment

Experienced clicker trained dogs are more likely to repeat a behaviour that has the reinforcement compared with the one that hasn't. If you begin with the youngster and guide them through the hunting exercises, you are continually reinforcing the flushing of the birds and renewed hunting. It is very unlikely at this young age that your dog will be successful in catching a rabbit. Be selective in your management of the situation; make sure the rabbits are fit and healthy in the area for hunting development.

If you do have a chase situation be careful not to introduce any level of approval from you for the chase; remain calm, quietly turn away and walk off in the opposite direction and find your own hunt. Yes, this takes courage!

As the dog rejoins you, collect them up and withdraw from the hunting area, taking time to bring your dog's level of arousal back to where they are cognitively aware of you. This is where the use of the lead is very effective but only if you have taught your dog to match pace and walk with you. This matching pace and walking together is a very good indicator that the dog is aware of the pack, in this case you. When they are again back in the cognitive level of the prey drive you can resume hunting.

I have seen my young dogs taught this very effectively by the older more experienced dogs. They will be hunting together and a youngster flushes a rabbit. The older dogs take no notice and continue searching for the game they perceive as of value to the hunt, the youngster does a racing start out of the blocks but no reinforcing back up from the rest of the group follows. The dog's brakes go on and you can almost physically see the sigh of embarrassment as the youngster rejoins the team. I am sure that if human they would be nonchalantly whistling under their breath in that 'who me?' way as they return.

The use of extinction in these circumstances can easily be transferred to other behaviours. In the chasing situation, begin with the small native birds that fly up in front of the young dog and are very tempting for them to follow. Use these tactics to transfer their attention to the real game to the exclusion of these. Then move on to rabbits. This may take a little longer but you have developed an excellent skill in your dog - the ability to use his or her initiative.

The dog will naturally begin to understand the importance of flushing against chasing as they gain experience.

BODY LANGUAGE

A dog's body language will tell us what drive it is in at any given time.

We can never assume to know what the dog is thinking, just learn to read the evidence of their body signs. For years I had successfully trained my dogs to work in the field as a team with me, never having heard of the term drives or modes, but teaching myself to pay attention to what they were telling me through the changes in their body language. Learning to anticipate when the change would happen and pre-empting it or just letting the dog have enough time to recover before allowing the work to continue. Also learning when to withdraw, not allowing the dog to reach the point of over stimulation, taking the dog away from the stimulus until its awareness is no longer impaired or as I often referred to it as 'the dogs brain has been re-engaged'. I think the correct terminology is cognitive functioning has no longer been impaired.

When hunting my dog's body language will be a mixture of

Excitement   Tails wag in a particular style

Heads held low or level for scenting	Travelling purposefully
Cast out exploring	Tightness to their muscles
Increased heart rate	Increased breathing rate
Single-minded, intent solely upon the task	

I do not think that the dog has an 'off' switch but learns to swap from one drive to another depending on the stimulus present. The majority of the stimuli that do this are associated with the environment. My dogs at home will be in pack drive, they relax, lazing in the chair or sun bathe in the conservatory but if I change my clothing to those used when shooting this stimulates them into action. The car drive swaps them into relaxation, but as soon as we arrive the field environment stimulates the swap to prey drive and work.

I was once asked what were the desirable traits in a hunting dog and one of the things I said was patience, this was frowned upon at the time I think for being slightly anthropomorphic, but on checking the definition and finding the inclusion of the phrases 'bearing trials calmly', and 'quality of endurance' I still believe it is correct.

A dog in prey drive will often continue through exhaustion and injury, and draw on reserves that have not been seen before in order to complete the job, those same reserves may well include patience. It takes a great skill, speed and strength to continually catch prey on the move, without 'patience' the technique of successful ambush would never be developed. Think of the dog that misses the rabbit as it pops its head out of the hole and then sits waiting for hours for it to reappear. Or the dog that sees the rabbit run across the field and instead of chasing cuts it off and heads for the hole where it waits for the rabbit to return, sometimes from sunrise to sunset.

Intertwined with patience is self control, these are the elements that we need and can build on with training. A dog that is in prey drive is still very capable of working through puzzles and in so doing will be able to control the urge to chase, they need to do this until the chance of successful capture is very high. Ultimately at the end of the day too much failure would put the group and their survival in jeopardy.

This self-control and patience is something that can be taught and developed. The concept is based upon this natural skill having these two qualities, following the set chains and links the job gets done successfully.

REWARDS

Some of the elements within a drive will naturally out weigh others. This is how we can develop our understanding of what our dog finds reinforcing, for some it will be the chase for others the scent and others the retrieve. Some of this will even have been encouraged possibly unintentionally in early learning. Take the desire to chase that has never resulted in the capture, in this case the dog was stimulated to chase but the capture and possession were never developed. The result is that the chase will outweigh the desire to complete the last two. This may be our dog that loves to run even after flushing the bird with no conception of returning to the scent, or the dog that enjoys the hunt but has no inclination to retrieve. Alternatively, by never achieving the capture following a chase the chase behaviour begins to extinguish. A good balance between all elements is needed.

Because our dogs are already working in this prey drive and ultimately doing what they find rewarding motivation is not a particular issue. Self-reward generates motivation and the motivation then finds the reward. The issues arise when we loose sight of the reward and what the dog is doing outweighs anything we can offer.

The motivation issue will arise when we take the dog into the pack drive to carry out the majority of the foundation and control training. This is where we need to develop and keep sight of the rewards we can use. With clicker training we have already begun to develop the dog's desire to work with us, this positive aspect of the training will help us to develop our partnership and rewards even further.

Food is also a valuable reward for us as it essentially forms part of the prey drive. It is the motivation that triggers the hunt. Its level of value we know depends on certain factors that differ from dog to dog but as clicker trainers we know how to increase its value and use it effectively as a tool. There are excellent recipes for this in both the Foundation and Novice books of the Clicker Trainer's Series from Learning About Dogs.

Play is another very useful reward and one that has not been developed to its full potential within this sport. It is an excellent way of re-adjusting the levels between the prey drive and pack drive. This is the way all dogs learn about all three drives, play teaches them how to hunt, how to communicate alongside social etiquette, and how to defend themselves and their resources.

By managing play, simulating games that utilise chase, and self-control we can teach the dogs the awareness of the pack. This will give them the skill to be able to swap quickly and respond to our stimulus control when hunting. This play should be developed as early as possible and will bring out the self-control we desire alongside, and at the same time, as the other skills and behaviours.

Build play into your training programme from the beginning, whether it is games with food or toys or just a great tug. Play is an excellent reward for concentration.

Excitability is something that I have never considered training into my dogs, the 'high drives' within the prey drive are already in place. These will then naturally come into play when the dog is hunting. My main consideration is to develop self-control and teach the dog to understand that by maintaining this control the work that is self-rewarding will ultimately follow. Excitability never enters the equation, as this mix will likely push the dogs over the point of being able to sustain self-control.

SELF-REWARDING BEHAVIOURS

A self-rewarding behaviour is one that does not need any reinforcement at the end of it; the process of doing it is reinforcing.

Behaviour that is not enjoyed will often be repeated because the reward follows and it is the anticipation of that reward that keeps it going. This does not make it self-rewarding. You know yourself if you have a chore to do at home that you dislike immensely, I think ironing is one of the most common, it will be completed if you plan for something desirable to follow, a treat such as a cream egg will do it for me. It does not make ironing itself reinforcing, but the completion of it. If I could watch my favourite Indiana Jones film on the TV at the same time as doing the ironing I would relish the ironing and even begin to anticipate doing it. The pleasure of watching the film becomes merged with the behaviour of ironing and thus it becomes self-rewarding.

We can use this in our training but first you need to identify what is a strong, self-rewarding behaviour for your dogs.

When Kemble is playing ball it is the chase of it that is rewarding, the bringing it back was of no consequence she would always return empty handed but focussed and ready in anticipation of another chase. For Thorn the capture and possession part of the ball after chase is rewarding, just being able to collect it up and carry it around was enough. Keeping the ball still is no good for any of them; it has to be bouncing or moving at speed otherwise they loose the focus and move on to something else. For some retrievers holding a suitable object for many hours is intensely satisfying.

All my Vizslas find having the wing passed across their noses pleasurable and it generate intense focus if used and then hidden. It is great for building the duration behaviour; this is based on utilising the scent drive from the hunting chain.

Our dogs have these base behaviours genetically ingrained as instincts and because of this we can utilise them very effectively and merge them with other behaviours to make them become self-rewarding. At the end of the day the dogs have been bred over hundreds of generations to find these activities self-rewarding and we have selected them because they do.

Some of the things that we can utilise include, tug playing, prey chasing, affection, attention, eating. One of the best for us to capture and put on cue is the scenting.

TUG GAMES

These are excellent games to teach your dog the skill of swapping from the prey drive into pack drive. To develop excellent self-control during very high levels of excitement and quick response to stimulus control. At the end of long spells of concentration or hard training sessions it provides a high value reward. There are lots of other reasons not least is its fun for both you and the dog.

These have always been avoided within this sport in the fear that they will teach the dog to bite hard on the game and cause damage. I think the biggest difficulty was that within the other methods of training there has never been the skill or ability to teach the dog the difference between tugging on toy rope and picking up a pheasant.

Clicker-trained dogs are skilled at reading contextual cues. The environment cues them to act and behave in certain ways. The dummies cue them to retrieve. The jump cues them to jump. The tug toy cues them to tug. The pheasant cues them to pick up with care.

I do play tug with my dogs, I always have, I have certain rules that we play by, I have special toys for tugging, and I only play tug in certain environments. I teach very clear and precise rules to the game to make it safe.

Since encouraging Kemble to play more tug games, it has strengthened her ability to retrieve and helped make the retrieve more reliable. By following the recipes in the retrieve chapter you will be shaping the dog to retrieve as a skill on its own and not relying on just their natural ability. This helps make the necessary adjustments so that they can do both.

There are lots of great recipes in the other books and an excellent article on tug training in *Teaching Dogs Magazine Vol 4 Issues 1 & 2.*

RECIPE: 15

CAPTURING SCENT AS SELF-REWARDING BEHAVIOUR

Find your dog's self rewarding behaviour, set it up and capture it, and put it on cue. Use both a visual and verbal cue, so that it can be used close by or at a distance from you, which is useful for encouraging the steadiness in the point for the HPR's. You will then be able to transfer the emotion of that behaviour to another behaviour.

1. Find somewhere that has a lot of birds or rabbits and allow the dog to take the scent in, settle with the dog and just let the scents flow over them.

2. Repeat this as often and as regularly as possible.

3. Watch for the dog to adopt the behaviours of absorbing the scent, they will likely become still, tilting their noses to the wind, there will be a slight tension about them, and their mouths will be slightly apart. I have also noticed that the dogs with a strong sense of scent will drool.

4. Put this on cue 'bliss'. Later you can then use this to click behaviours that your dog does not find rewarding, like for example sitting 'waiting'.

5. Refresh this cue regularly to keep it robust, take the dog to where the scent is and ask them to do the behaviour you have been using it to reinforce, like the 'waiting' and let the actual scent merge with the behaviour. Cue the wait and then cue the 'bliss'.

For us the use of the food and scent can also be paired with many other actions such as the recall, the searching, and jumping. Shaking can be paired with the retrieve delivery from water.

STIMULUS VERSUS CONTROL

The battle of stimulus versus control is not exclusive to the shooting field. In many dog related activities the stimuli that arouse the natural instinct can quickly exceed the handler's stimulus control. In the beginning the field stimulus is huge in comparison to the level of control. As experience grows with the dog and behaviours are taken through planned training exercises this gradually changes and the effect of the stimuli decrease and the level of control increases.

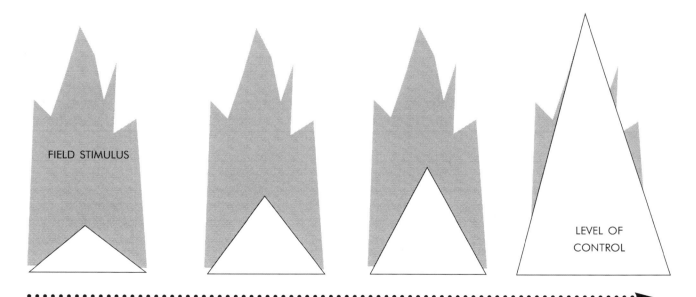

QUANTITY OF TRAINING AND EXPERIENCE

The major difficulties for both dog and handler arise in the shooting environment. Stimulation can present itself in many different forms: visual, mental, scent, noise and very often simultaneously. This stimulation not only affects the dog but also the handler. Excitement builds in the handler who can easily lose concentration and transfer this to the dog. This then results in a less than perfect experience.

Visual stimulation will include:

Activity of other dogs	Quantity of game
Number of people	Flight of the birds
Running of the ground game	Hand signals as cues

Scent stimulation will include:

Other dogs	Driven game
Other game	Other people

Noise stimulation will include:

People with guns	The keeper
Beaters with dogs	Other beaters
Picking up dogs and handlers	Whistles
Flags	Hunting horns
Sticks banging on trees	Birds 'cocking up'
Feathers whistling as they take off	Ground game squeaking
Hooves as the deer run through	Clothing rustling
Wind	Whistle signals as cues
Verbal signals as cues	

To the inexperienced the noise level on a commercial shoot can be overwhelming.

Taste stimulation will include:

> The taste from the game retrieved

MENTAL STIMULATION

The mental stimulation will vary and depends on the experience of the dog. Dogs that have been highly bred for shooting will often respond to the stimuli and without any prior experience will recognise instantly the potential of the environment. The impact this has on them will then change as experience grows.

It is hardly surprising that both handler and dog can have the hunting drive aroused to the point of exclusion of all else.

Experience can grow in two ways:

1. To the benefit of the working partnership by improving self-control in relation to the stimulus.

2. To the detriment of the partnership where the dog's experience in the situation has outweighed the handler's level of stimulus control, result is 'the dog knows best', the hunting drives take over and nothing else has an impact except catching the game at the end of the hunt.

I do not believe there is such a thing as a disobedient dog. Dogs need to be able to maintain enormous self-control in the presence of such overwhelming stimulus. The dog does what it believes are the required behaviours at that time under those circumstances. This is the result of the handler not taking enough time to build sufficient strength and control into the behaviours before taking them to this level.

Our aim is to reach a level where the controlling stimulus is always one level higher than any other stimulus for the dog.

STIMULUS

The definition of a stimulus is an 'act to arouse action' therefore it is anything that gets a response from the dog. It can be any of the things mentioned above plus an instinctive response to a drive. They can happen individually or sometimes as described all at once. They can happen externally or internally.

We know that our dogs will instantly respond to the scent of the game in a particular pattern of behaviours but in the wrong environment when perhaps training another behaviour this will then become a distraction. This distraction is likely to decrease the response time in relation to the behaviour or the dog may even be unable to complete the behaviour at all. The majority of distractions trigger unwanted responses as far as we are concerned. What we require at the end of the day is the majority of distractions to not trigger any response. The dog needs to be able to file these distractions as *"no need to respond"*. We can also use distraction to break concentration; if the dog is focussed on something other than the job at hand we will often use ourselves as the distraction to break their focus. Finding your own things to hunt will fit into this category.

Finally, our cues are a learned stimulus used in association with specific behaviours. They trigger desirable behaviours that we reward. These cues the dogs need to file as *"need to respond"*. Cues can become distractions if they have significance to the dog, for example the sound of gunshot relates to the possibility of the retrieval of game and triggers the dog into active response. What we actually desire in this situation are the dogs to acknowledge the sound of the shot and prepare themselves to mark the retrieve but not instantly leap into action to do the job. We need the dog to file this as a cue for *"possible response"* after a second (learned) cue.

TEACHING CONCENTRATION AND FOCUS

In order to achieve all this we need to teach the dog the skills

To respond   Not to respond   Respond in a minute

To teach the dog these skills we need to

- ▶ Understand how much impact each type of stimulus has on our dog

- ▶ How proximity to the stimulus affects our dog

- ▶ At what point arousal exceeds the reinforcement for the behaviour

RECIPE 16

TEACHING FOCUS

The default to look for cues from you

This is an excellent base on which to begin to build your control work. Teach the dog to focus on you so that they can easily listen for your cues, respond to them and carry them out as you have trained them. You will need to teach them to be focussed on you at any time and from any distance. They may not actually be looking at you but they will be aware of you and expecting some form of direction, another cue, or some reassurance that they are working well that gives them the confidence to continue working away from you.

When you begin choose an area with a surface that the dog can easily see thrown pieces of food, indoors or on clean ground. Thrown food in grass is very difficult to see and takes an experienced dog to find it without hunting. You can adapt this for outdoor training with "reward stations", such as a small flat mat or tray that will contain the delivered food. This behaviour will become the 'default', i.e.: the behaviour the dog will adopt when no other cue is forthcoming. The absence of a cue, *is* the cue for this behaviour.

1. Throw several pieces of food to the floor click as the dog eats each piece.

2. When the last piece has gone, wait for the dog to finish hunting (just in case there are some left that they missed), and as soon as the dog looks at you '*any more then?*' click and reward this decision and throw another piece of food to the floor.

3. In order for it to become the first thought in the dog's mind when nothing else has been cued, you must repeat this behaviour hundreds of times. When there is a break in the process, or the dog simply couldn't hear your cue or is not sure what you have cued they will revert to this behaviour.

4. Always throw the food to the floor, making sure you click for the look to you.

5. This becomes a measure of your dog's ability to cope with levels of either stimuli or stress in particular environments. If the dog is unable to look to you in this simple behaviour then the stimuli are exceeding the dog's ability to focus and further cues will be wasted.

6. Gradually increase the criteria so that it becomes more difficult for the dog to find you. Throw the food behind obstacles, or upon surfaces, and move or turn away as the dog goes off to get the food. When they look for you, you are in a different location and they have to actively locate your face.

7. Introduce other distractions such as moving people. This will mimic a busy shoot and give the dog a foundation skill of being able to "find" you when returning from a retrieve. The shooting field can resemble a busy shopping arcade on a Saturday, as beaters, dogs, guns, keepers are all milling about with accompanying noise, game and dogs.

My dogs are very good at transferring this "awareness of me" behaviour from home to field hunting.

SWITCH OFF - RELAX

When the focus is not required, teach the dog how to relax, or switch down.

Begin with the dog on lead, which acts as the temporary cue, and cue the dog to settle. Make specific changes in your body language, the way you are relaxed but standing and this will become the field cue. More of this is discussed in **MATCHING PACE** *page 79.*

Our dogs are able to transfer this to the situation as required. Thorn often works on the peg with my husband and can instantly tell when he should be focussed and 'on duty' and when to relax, sometimes he will lie down at his side. He picks this up from the way my husband stands, how he holds the gun and often if he is talking (on the phone !) this is a great indication for a spell of time out. The youngster has picked this up very quickly as well. The dogs are allowed to choose their relaxed behaviour during these times, which is far more beneficial to their well being than a directly cue a specific behaviour. Sometimes you can be waiting for half an hour in position at the start of a drive while the keeper pushes the birds in. I have known the dogs lie and take in the sun when waiting for a drive to start. It is also a good indication of their ability to swap from prey drive into pack drive and their levels of self-control.

Take time to teach the dog the food games from the **SIT AND MARK** Recipe 44 *page 122* in the Chapter 5 Retrieve Training. This will also teach your dog to focus on the 'rabbit' to the exclusion of all other distractions.

RECIPE: 17

SQUEAL MEANS JOIN ME

Using a distraction as a cue to focus on you

It is not uncommon to hear a squealing rabbit or hare in the field, which is one of the most powerful cues for a hunting dog to join the cooperative kill. This exercise teaches the dog to file this noisy event in the 'not worth responding' to compartment.

1. Finding a good squeaky toy that your dog is interested in. Condition the squeak to food:

   Squeak the toy and feed the dog   Squeak the toy and feed the dog
   Squeak the toy and feed the dog   Squeak the toy and feed the dog
   Squeak the toy and feed the dog

   Squeak with left hand shove food with right, even if you need to push the food to the dog's mouth.

2. Repeat this more than 30 times.

3. Put the toy out of sight under your foot and repeat the exercise again.

4. Very gradually change from shoving the food at the dog to allowing them to take it. Make the change one inch at a time.

5. Increase the distance so that when the dog hears the squeak they have to make a physical movement towards your hand for the food. Hold the food out after the squeak. We now have squeak followed by offered food, visible movement to take food.

6. Introduce the clicker and mark the movement towards your now empty hand that is triggered by the squeak. Collect a piece of food to deliver to the dog.

   This has now changed from: Squeak - Feed

   to   Squeak - Look at You - Collect Food

   (marked with the click)

7. Increase the criteria by tossing the food so that the dog has to travel further to reach you on the next squeak.

8. Introduce lots of different squeaks; different locations make the behaviour flexible.

PROFILING YOUR DOG

In order to understand how all these factors will affect your dog you need to build up a base profile. This can then be used to read the changes in body language that will help you to manage the stimuli, know when the arousal level will be at the point where it excludes all else, and prevent you from crossing this point.

You will understand when your dog is focussed, when they are aware of you, how much impact everything around them is having on a particular behaviour. It will also provide you with evidence to know when the dog is ready and experienced enough to move on to the next level.

RECIPE: 18

MEASURING FITNESS AND EXCITEMENT LEVELS

The heart rate will vary with exercise, excitement and stress. It will also increase with pain, early stages of shock, and electric shock. The breathing rate increases dramatically after exercise or play.

MEASURING THE PULSE

Dogs' heart rates vary from 60 to 160 beats per minute. Large athletic dogs have slower rates than small dogs and puppies. Puppies rates can be as high as 200 beats per minute.

1. Monitor the pulse by placing the fingers inside the hind leg where it joins the body. Move the fingers around until the pulse is found.

2. Count the beats over 20 seconds and multiply by three for the rate per minute. Do not apply too much pressure, as the pulse will disappear.

MEASURE THE BREATHING

Dogs normally breath between 10 and 30 times a minute. Small breeds and young dogs breathe more quickly than large or mature ones.

1. Visually count the number of breaths in 20 seconds, multiply by 3 to find the rate per minute.

Begin by making a record of your dog's pulse rate in the following situations these will form your control base.

1. When they are relaxed at home

2. When they are out free running but aware of your presence

3. When out in an environment of high level stimulation, *for example: close to a pen of game birds but with no other activity taking place*

4. When they are out in the environment that is the most stimulating for them, *for example: on the edge of a shoot on a shoot day*

	Relaxed	Free running	High Stimulation	Max Stimulation
Pulse Rate				
Breathing Rate				

At different stages during your training programme retake them and make comparisons. If the levels are gradually dropping, for example, if the rate at 2 (free running) is getting closer to the control at 1 (relaxed) and rate 3 (high stimulation) is getting closer to 2 then your training programme is progressing well and you can increase the levels of stimulation for your behaviours.

RECIPE: 19

MEASURING THE EFFECT OF THE STIMULI

The different types and intensity of stimuli will affect each dog in different ways. You need to be able to measure the effect that a particular stimulus, at a particular level, will have on your dog and use it to decide when to increase the criteria or difficulty.

▶ Complete the questionnaire in Appendix B *page 159* to establish your stimuli levels for each dog.

▶ Each location change will have an impact and your control should be in the location that has the least such as the living room.

The proximity and focus questions are designed to find out if the dog has yet developed the skill of checking in and will help you be able to manage the dog. From this you can gauge if the dog has any cognitive awareness of your presence. If it hasn't then there isn't much point in trying to move on.

The question for noise level gives an indication of the level of arousal within the dog and how it might try to release some of this. A colleague who works cockers has one little chap that by choice never sits. He is quite able to manage himself and maintain excellent self-control as long as he is standing. All the time his tail never stops wagging, not in a slow way but the manic helicopter type. When asked to sit it was observed that he could not wag his tail in the same manner, and although he maintained his self-control he began to whine. The tail wagging is a stress release, take that away and he had to find another less desirable way to release it - whining.

With the sight-blocking test use a clip board in front of the dog or place your hands over their eyes. This is a very good measure of how bothered the dog is by the stimulus level present and how much trust in you they have.

Over arousal is the level at which the stimulus has exceeded a point where the behaviour deteriorates or reinforcement is ineffective. This is measured in questions 7 and 8. If the dog cannot eat, or the behaviour deteriorates then the dog's arousal is too high and you need to drop the level of stimulus and/or criteria. Use only simple behaviours here such as sit, down, target hand.

Some examples of stimuli to test are

Other dogs watching	TV	Wild birds
Food being served	Other people	Children
Doorbell	Outside	Inside

Different locations outside   Other dogs playing   Other dogs working

Scent

Take the time to analyse the shooting environment, make a list of the entire stimuli that may trigger the dog and become unwanted cues, or take the dog into a state of over arousal. Work these stimuli into your training programme and teach the dog to file them in the correct compartment.

Using the pheasant and rabbit pens are excellent ways of setting up controllable situations for working through control exercise or building focus and strength into behaviours.

RECIPE: 20

TESTING CONTROL AGAINST THE ENVIRONMENT

Once you have completed several questionnaires against a variety of stimuli in different locations you can build this into your training programme and move on to testing the dog's level of control against the environment.

Each time you change either a stimulus or the type of environment you will need to test each behaviour again.

I have established a list of stimuli and environments and scored them from the questionnaire. Some examples:

FOR RIOJA IN GARDEN:

Dogs watching scores level	1	People scores level	1
Food served scores level	5	Dogs playing scores level	5
Wild Birds scores level	1		

FOR RIOJA IN FIELD

Dogs watching scores level	1	People scores level	1
Food served scores level	5	Dogs playing scores level	5
Wild birds scores level	5		

To test the sit I repeat 10 repetitions of the behaviour in the control location in the garden. One level of stimulus is introduced beginning with the lowest and building until I can introduce as many variations as possible without losing the quality of the behaviour. I use repetitions of 10 to give a clear measurement of the fluency and strength of the behaviour at that time. If the behaviour breaks down within a batch of ten then it certainly will not withstand any further introduction of stimuli. The scores are recorded so that I can then refer back to if a behaviour begins to deteriorate.

The score for the behaviour strength is between 1 & 3:

0 = the behaviour did not happen at all

1= the behaviour was weak in both memory and physical skill

2= the behaviour was weak in either memory or physical skill

3= the behaviour was strong in both memory and physical skill

The success rate should be 100% if below this you should not introduce another stimulus. If your success rate remains at 100% then you begin to introduce your stimulus one at a time with the lowest levels first. So for the behaviour sit I would then introduce a level 1 stimulus such as other dogs watching. Build up to 100 % then introduce another stimulus so people plus other dogs watching build back up again.

These are the results for Rioja at 18 months old. The behaviour under test was the sit, the control location - the garden. Reward ratio is 1:1 (one reward for one behaviour)

No of repetitions	Control	Control + Level 1	Control + 2 x Level 1	Control + Level 5	Control + Level 5 + Level 1
1	3	3	3	3	3
2	3	3	3	3	3
3	3	3	3	3	3
4	3	3	3	2	2
5	3	3	3	2	2
6	3	3	3	3	2
7	3	3	3	3	2
8	3	3	3	3	2
9	3	3	3	3	2
10	3	3	3	3	2
% Success at 3	100%	100%	100%	80%	*30%

Stimulus Level 1 = other dogs watching

Stimulus Level 1 = people watching

Stimulus Level 5 = other dogs playing

*With a success level this low there would be no point in moving on.

At level 1 control your behaviour should be of top quality, fluent and only happens when cued before you start.

As your dog becomes more experienced in these exercises the levels of stimulus and the number of stimulus combinations will increase quicker. Your experience at reading the dog and the dogs growing experience of working in the different environments will ultimately build towards a 100% success rate.

When your simple behaviours are 100% reliable then you can change the control level again and begin to introduce combinations of behaviours to be tested. For example: sit in front, working up to combinations such as stop at 30 feet, recall and retrieve.

You are aiming to achieve 100% success rate on any cued behaviour in a location such as a pheasant pen with birds.

RECIPE: 21

TARGET BACK OF HAND TO MEASURE CONTROL

Here is an exercise using a simple, but strong behaviour.

1. Remind your dog of the behaviour, repeat 10 on a 1:1 reward basis.

2. Introduce food as a distraction. Holding food in your left hand, toss a piece of the food further out to your left, and give the "touch hand" signal with your right hand. The dog has to pass the food hand to touch the hand, click and reward on a 1:1 basis.

3. Repeat this until the dog can achieve a success rate of 10 out of 10.

4. Place the food on a chair, and position your hand so that the dog has to pass the food on the chair to touch it, build again until 10 out of 10. You must not introduce any other cues; this is purely on the strength of your target hand behaviour versus the distraction of the food.

5. Place the food on the floor and repeat as above.

6. Change the distance of the food from the target hand.

7. Change the distance the dog has to travel to reach the target hand from the food.

8. Then change the location and begin right back at step 1 and continue to build the behaviour up until you reach step 7 again.

9. Repeat this changing location until the dog can achieve the top quality behaviour at step 7 in a pen full of pheasants.

You can do this exercise with any number of combinations of behaviours and distractions, use a toy, introduce noise, roll a ball that equates to the visual stimulation from fleeing prey and will likely trigger the chase. It is often the rapid movement in the peripheral vision that is the strongest trigger. This is a good use for the bolting rabbit but watch that elastic!

RECIPE: 22

USING CAGED BIRDS TO DEVELOP SELF-CONTROL AND STIMULUS CONTROL

If you have decided to keep some birds for training purposes, or have access to some from a local shoot or supplier, then these can also be used to develop self-control and stimulus control. This is especially effective for puppies, young dogs, and older dogs without much experience but that are very 'hunty'. Their hunting drive is developing much quicker and stronger than the self-control.

Take a bird, or birds, and put them in a cage that is of a suitable size and can easily be moved about. Begin in an area of least distraction, such as a garage or garden shed. Make sure you have records of your dog's pulse and breathing rates and have taken a completed record from the questionnaire.

This exercise will also begin to teach the skill of eating (taking your reward) to an older dog that due to the levels of arousal is at present unable to eat when training in close proximity to game.

1. Introduce your dog to the birds, carry out the tests on the questionnaire (Appendix B *page 159*) and take the pulse and breathing rates, make a note of the results give this stimulus a score.

2. Continue to introduce your dog on a daily basis to the birds, taking a record of the test results until your dog can eat one piece of food when with them and the pulse and breathing rates have begun to drop.

3. Pick a simple behaviour such as hand target or sit, and begin working with this behaviour on a 1:1 reward basis in the presence of the birds. The first time you may only get one response to cue. That's great stuff, just take your time and build up gradually to ten repetitions. If you are only able to get one response to cue at this time to something as simple and well conditioned as the 'sit', what chance have you in achieving success with a more complex behaviour such as 'stop' when this close to game out in the field?

4. Build the behaviour back to top quality performance.

5. As your dog begins to develop the skill of managing itself in this environment, introduce more varieties of simple behaviours followed by more complex ones, and lastly simple chains.

6. Then take your cage of birds to more challenging environments.

7. When your dog can reliably and comfortably eat in the majority of varied situations with the fluent behaviours re-introduce the dog to hunting in controlled environments.

SUSTAINING A BEHAVIOUR

This is a mental exercise in self-control. Puppies find it much harder than older dogs, since they are more stimulated by the novelty of their environments.

There are two types of sustained behaviour that you will need to teach your dog:

▶ the alert, poised for action, sit needed for work on the peg with the gun, whilst waiting for the retrieve cue

▶ the relaxed down, which is useful for teaching the dog to relax at lunchtime.

It is for you to decide how long you will need the behaviour to be sustained for and whether or not you will need the dog to stay out of sight. It may be useful to teach them this skill, since at some shoots you may have to enter the shooting lodge to collect your lunch, without your dog.

Be aware that for some dogs maintaining these positions in close proximity to other dogs is stressful in itself, but to be there and alone when you are out of sight is much worse. You will need to teach this very gradually, building the dog's confidence in being alone, you must do this with care and empathy otherwise you will cause lasting damage to the relationship. For this dog the stay is a 'punishment'.

Teach the dog to understand that for these exercises the food will be delivered to them instead of the usual tossing that they are used to. The delivery method of the food will reinforce the 'stillness' in the position. I use a quieter clicker for this one to indicate "relax the food is coming" which helps reduce the initial 'alertness' that is always present with the normal clicker followed by the toss of the food. The quiet click will also signify your return to deliver the food, a double reward.

The dogs will easily be able to transfer this learning to other behaviours.

RECIPE: 23

THE DOWN STAY

It is easier to teach the stay behaviour in the down position and then transfer it to a sit. You can use the same 'stay' cue for both behaviours.

1. Teach the dog a relaxed stay in the down position, use the settle position, which is with one hip dropped to the side, relaxed joints. Consistently use the same hip dropped for this behaviour and feed the dog to this side behind their front leg.

2. When you click make sure you have the food ready to instantly reward in the position. Have a reserve of food ready in your hand, and repeat rapidly 30 times.

3. Position yourself so that you are standing in front of the dog, make sure you do not have to lean towards the dog to deliver the food. You should be relaxed yourself. Slowly build the gap between the delivery of the food and the next click after the first 30 repetitions.

4. Then build the gap between the click and the delivery. This will teach the dog to stay in the position while waiting for the click and then on hearing the click to also stay still. You will need this when you begin to increase the distance.

5. Build strength and reliability into the behaviour and add your 'stay' cue.

RECIPE: 24

THE SIT STAY

1. Make sure you have a good clean upright sit and that the dog is comfortable before you start. If not the dog is more likely to 'need' to readjust and you want to set them up for complete success right from the start.

2. Repeat the steps as for the down stay.

Once you have reached step 5 in either behaviour you will then need to introduce your distractions and increase criteria to build durability into the behaviour.

Make a list of these changes and introduce one at a time, if you increase too fast do not worry just drop back a level as you would with any other behaviour and build back up again. Make sure all the changes you make are gradual and the dog will be able to maintain the position without difficulty.

Leave extreme changes, such as turning your back, until after the behaviour has been tested against less disengaging body language. Remember to include:

- ▶ waving your arms about, this will prepare the dog for when you begin to throw dummies.

- ▶ run around, this is a great way to begin to increase self-control against movement. It encourages the dog to understand that not all movement warrants a reaction.

- ▶ flying birds and dummy throwing

- ▶ dummy launching.

When you feel the dog is ready take to a shoot and build the final part of the distraction into the behaviour. Ask the keeper if you can work with your dog behind the pickers up, remember you are working on stays here and not retrieve. Use the opportunity to proof through the birds flying, dropping, and all the other distractions that are present. This will be your final test of the behaviour before its ready to build into chains and take into the field.

Always return to the dog to feed, when you return begin to count to three before delivering the food. Remain calm when you teach this exercise avoid introducing excitement at the end. Use the food to reward this as the dog will anticipate the greater rewards and may begin to move towards you or get excited and start fidgeting.

Introduce another cue to release the dog after the last piece of food, such as your 'get on', target hand 'touch', or a walk at close. Remember to reinforce this, as the stay behaviour has a high reinforcement history in comparison.

The dog must be able to relax when you are in view before you begin to develop the out of sight behaviour. Gradually moving out of sight behind the dog, into the blind spot, anticipate the dog turning to look for you and get your click in before this happens. Take a long time to build this part of the behaviour, as this will be the best foundation for teaching the dog to stay when you are out of sight. Build the out of sight behaviour very gradually, taking one step at a time, allow the dog to use its senses to 'know' that you are still close by. Use the wind for carrying your scent when you go out of sight, so that the dog is fully aware of your location.

MATCHING PACE

When a pack goes out to hunt they are most in tune with each other, varying their pace to either keep up or drop back. They are very aware of any slight changes in direction made by any member. A purposeful change in direction or intensity in hunting body language will trigger a response in the other pack members. This is the cue to "join up" the hunt has begun. The ability to react to this could mean the difference between a successful kill or a failed hunt and the pack is in jeopardy.

Our biggest problem is that we do not move fast enough on the hunt for the dog. When left to move at their own pace they usually trot out in a nice relaxed way covering quite a distance at a good speed. This is not our idea of the pace for the hunt. We would find it very difficult to match this natural speed and maintain it over any distance. The first thing the dog has to be able to do is to adjust itself to this new speed for the hunt.

This skill is so important we must teach it correctly right from the start. It is a great measure of their ability to maintain self-control and work cooperatively. It can also be used to teach them to relax at certain times when they are working. I will always use a lead when taking a young dog out working. I usually put the dog on a lead between drives, this is a cue to them that nothing is about to happen and helps them regain their self control and reserves ready for the next drive. The removal of the lead is then the cue to be ready to go to work.

To teach the dog to walk on a loose lead and match pace with me I use an ordinary plain collar and a six-foot long lead with an elasticated handle. This handle I find helps take the impact should the dog lunge or run to the end.

Begin with the attitude that the walk belongs to you; it is not the dog's right to be there, puppies and young dogs are left behind in the den until they are useful to either the hunt or patrol. The pup follows the pack; they certainly don't wander around everywhere after the puppies every whim.

The walk itself is very rewarding to the dog. They can enjoy every aspect of a hunt, or patrol as if they were free, they can sniff scents, mark, check where the game is or where the good looking girl from next door has been. All this will give them heaps of pleasure and you can be the manager of this pleasure. As long as they follow the rules all these things will follow.

RECIPE: 25

LOOSE LEAD WALKING

Decide which side you want your dog to work on and keep to this side. They will be able to swap sides later but to make the learning easier for them teach one side consistently. I will use the left side for the purposes of this recipe.

Take the lead in your right hand, put your hand through the loop and grip the base of the handle in your palm. Pass the lead loosely across the front of your body; take hold of the lead in your left hand. Make sure there is slack lead going from this hand to the dog's collar. This will later become the cue for the dog to be in the correct location.

Begin in the lowest area of distraction you can find and then gradually build it up. I have a quiet farm track that the dogs know well and I can use to begin building this behaviour. It is just wide enough for the hedges to be a distraction but not close enough that I can't move away effectively if needs be. There is little traffic to cause a major nuisance but enough to help build on this. Grasp these basic principles first and then tackle the distractions. Sometimes it will feel as though you are going backwards but don't worry take your time things will improve again. Remember to keep ownership of the walk.

1. Begin by teaching the dog to stand still next to you, click and reward the dog for standing there, feed the dog from hand, you are creating the feeling within the dog that this place beside you is a very good place to be. If the dog is unable to stand still by your side then they definitely will not be able to walk by it.

2. Use your body language to let the dog know this is your walk, stand up straight but relax your shoulders let your arms drop by your sides. Do this exercise as silently as possible let the dog work out from your body language, the click and reward what is happening. The silence from you will teach them to be aware of you through each stride. The dog must understand from you that it is your walk.

3. Once the dog can stand still by your side you can then set off. Do not rush, begin walking quite slowly, the faster you go will encourage the dog to speed up.

4. When, or if, the dog goes away ahead of you, stop, release your left hand and take hold of the elastic handle with both hands and lean slightly back ready to take up the force from the pull. Do not move, stand quite still. The walk has ended, wait for them to look at you, and gently guide them back directly to your left side. Do not pull them back and do not allow them to go round the back of you.

5. Introduce a click for the look back at you, and feed when back by your side. You will have to practise holding the clicker on the lead handle and to make sure that your thumb is off it when the dog goes out to the end of the lead. You do not want to inadvertently 'click' the pull.

6. When the dog is back by your side stay standing still, do not move straight off take the slack of the lead in your left hand again and count to ten. By introducing this pause and count of ten you will prevent building a chain and teaching your dog to be a yo-yo on the end of the lead. It gives the dog time to relax at your side, and for you to gather the walk back into your domain.

7. If the dog stays still by your side then move off again slowly. Keep repeating this until the dog demonstrates they can walk level with you. Some dogs will get it straight away others will take a little longer.

8. Change the timing of the click to match the dog's decision to move back towards you unaided.

9. If your dog moves off sideways from you to sniff the hedge or lamppost then readjust yourself away from it by taking a few steps in the opposite direction.

10. Avoid turning round in a circle with your dog at the end of the lead. Manage the lead and stand still.

11. If your dog takes no notice when at the end of the lead then give it a shake and make yourself a nuisance until they notice you and if necessary once they acknowledge you take a step backwards.

12. Put behaviours such as sniffing the hedges and posts and peeing on cue. You will then be able to use them as a reward for good walking 'go sniff'. Peeing on cue will mean that you can manage when and where this happens. Link the peeing on cue with the additional cue of the lead. This avoids unwanted eliminating during work, and you can ensure your dog is empty before they begin.

13. Keep the lead loose and without tension, this will teach the dog to be relaxed and comfortable, a tight lead will likely put them on alert and expect trouble.

RECIPE: 26

USING FOOD AS A DISTRACTION TO TEACH SELF-CONTROL WHEN LEAD WALKING

Obtain a large piece of mat or old carpet cut into a square that can be used to place a pile of food on. Place the mat out a fair distance from you making sure the dog is aware that the food is on it. Begin to slowly walk towards the mat, apply the principles from the loose lead-walking recipe above. If the dog moves ahead stop still and wait for the dog to re join you. Wait and then set off again. Gradually get closer to the food making sure the dog is matching pace with you all the time. The reward for the dog is being able to get closer to the food. You can click for maintaining the position and pace with you and reward with a step closer to the food.

Be careful when you get very close to the mat that the dog doesn't lunge out and self-reward on the food. Manage this with the lead, when the dog can stand still by your side in very close proximity to the food, click this behaviour introduce a 'take it' cue and allow the dog to reward on the food pile. Build on this gradually and when your dog begins to show inhibition when approaching the food on the mat click this behaviour and cue take it. This is teaching the dog to inhibit itself in the presence of a strong stimulus. This is much better that using loss of reward to teach 'leave' as this is often associated with avoidance. Attach a cue 'stop' to the inhibition that is self-control. Introduce this cue when you can anticipate the inhibition will happen.

You can apply this same principle to teaching the dog not to go through the gate, doorway, or jump out of the car unless cued. Begin with the door open and the dog managed on a lead. Either clip the lead to the dog guard in the back of the car or stand on the end when by the door. Wait for the dog to withdraw from trying to get through click this behaviour and either throw the food to the dog in the car or feed from hand at the door. Once the dog has learned the skill of inhibiting itself from going through, or jumping out, introduce cues for the behaviours as required. Then you will need to gradually shut the doors and make sure that the opening of them does not become a new cue to go through, this is just taking the behaviours through the process of proofing.

RECIPE: 27

PARKING THE DOG

Teach the dog the skill of being able to relax by your side while out on a walk. This is a very useful tool for managing the dog when you are out in the field. Especially if you think that the levels of arousal are becoming too high and the dog is loosing that awareness of you. Change your body language at the same time to adopt a position of relaxation as opposed to ready to go. Stand with one hip dropped and shoulders down. This will teach the dog the difference between 'on' and 'off' duty when working. Allow the dog to watch what's going on and take it in.

▶ Take hold of the dog's collar with your left hand

▶ Allow the slack from the lead to drop down to the floor, whilst still holding the handle

▶ Put your foot firmly on the lead on the ground; make sure this is the foot that takes your weight. Make sure the length of the lead allows the dog to stand up straight, but not so long to allow the dog to jump.

▶ Let go of the dog's collar and hold the lead by the handle in your right hand

▶ Relax together and just watch the world go by

RECIPE: 28

WALKING FREE BY YOUR SIDE

The dog must be able to walk on a loose lead, maintain that position without error in areas of high stimulation.

The dog must have a good recall (page 30 & 34).

The principle is exactly the same as for teaching the matching pace on a lead. The dog maintains the pace and location by your side until you cue otherwise. I use the cue 'stay close' to re-establish the walk by my side and the cue 'get on' to release them. If the dog moves out of position without cue, I stop and wait until they bring themselves back, stand still for the count of ten, cue 'stay close' and set off. You can only do this if you have taught the dog the behaviour on lead first, otherwise the opportunity for self reward can arise from breaking the position. If you are in doubt, or the area is not entirely safe, attach a very light line to the dogs collar, so light that they believe they are off lead, but you have a back up in the case of their error. You can click for maintaining the pace and location by your side and reward with the continued walk or feed if you wish.

You will then need to strengthen this behaviour against all your levels of stimulation building up gradually to walking with you on the shoot.

All these exercises are designed to help you teach your dog awareness of you, self-control in the presence of extreme stimulation, when to respond to distraction, when to ignore it, and when to note it for appropriate response when required. This coupled with experience and the teaching of the specific skills will establish a true working partnership between you and your dog. Take your time with these skills they are the backbone of your training. Get it right in the beginning and you will have many years in which to enjoy the benefits.

4 Hunt Training

'I'm going to hunt'

Hunting is a basic instinct, a genetically ingrained set of behaviours for the dogs. Their skills have been honed over thousands of years and it is a wonderful experience to work in partnership with them.

WHAT IS THE HUNT?

It is a chain of behaviours clearly linked to each other where instinct 'drives' the dog to move from one link to the next.

The chain includes:

Hunt → Search → Locate → Approach → Pause → Pounce → Chase → Catch → Kill → Carry → Consume

For the field sport dog this natural chain of behaviours will be shaped, breaking them off at certain points and re-directed into other skills.

The pause has been developed into the point behaviour for the HPR's and Pointers & Setters:

Hunt → Search → Locate → Approach → Pause (on point)/

└──────►Drop → Flush

The pounce is the point in the chain that is broken and interim skills introduced such as the drop to flush.

The chase, catch and kill have been refined, and to some extent will be removed for the dog and carried out by the gun. Carry and consume is developed into the retrieve. This will be the working hunting chain as opposed to the natural chain described above.

Working Chain:

Hunt → Search → Locate → Approach → Point → Drop → Flush (Gun Shot) → Retrieve

Our part in this hunting process is also to build a partnership with the dog, to engage in the role with purpose, take this natural skill, enhance it and use it to enrich our relationship while at the same time taking on board the responsibilities that go with the job.

The working hunt chain will always result in a number of variables and there will be very little consistency in how this will occur. The hunt at the point of pounce can be broken off and either re-directed towards further hunting, a retrieve or a recall. This 'un-predictability' is probably our best tool in the kit, utilised to our advantage keeping the dog from learning to anticipate the next behaviour or building longer chains that will inevitably eventually return to the original natural chain.

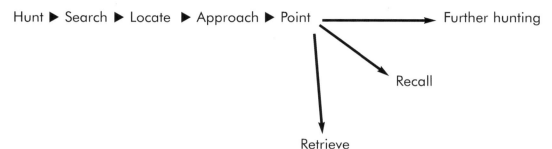

Hunt ▶ Search ▶ Locate ▶ Approach ▶ Point ⟶ Further hunting

Recall

Retrieve

For the flushing dogs the hunt chain you teach will go as follows:

SET OFF →

→ Quarter on wind and scent to locate game

→ Move onto game to flush

→ Drop on flush and wait

→ Use sight, wind and scent to locate retrieve

→ Return and deliver

For the HPR's the hunting chain you will teach will go as follows:

SET OFF →

→ Quarter on wind and scent to locate quarry

→ Point on quarry

→ Remain steady on point

→ Move forward to flush on cue

→ Drop on flush and wait

→ Use sight, wind; scent to locate retrieve

→ Return and deliver

The Retriever's chain you teach will go as follows:

SET OFF →

> → Use sight, the wind and scent to locate retrieve
>
> > → Return and deliver

It is important to make sure that you observe your dog to establish which part of the hunting chain they perceive as rewarding. This is important when later developing the longer chain and introducing the controlled behaviours. You will need to understand what you can use to reinforce the click. Each dog will be different so begin watching at the very beginning when first introducing your dog to the environment and game. Take notes these will be useful later on. Some examples are

- ▶ Hunting can be the motivation for the retrieve and the retrieve then reinforces (clicks) the hunting.

- ▶ The chase of the rabbit reinforces (clicks) the hunting.

- ▶ The jump after the bird reinforces (clicks) the flush and the scent of the bird can be the motivation for the hunt.

For some dogs it is the actual running itself that is reinforcing. The dog carries on after the flush just running to and fro across the field, long after the bird has long gone.

A dog that has no motivation to hunt is a dog that

1. Has no understanding of what hunting is.

2. Has not made the connection between the scent and the game.

3. Has been allowed too many false scents where nothing has been located.

4. Has been allowed to run on too long without finding game on bare ground causing the dog to:

> slow down and conserve energy or
>
> value the running more than the scenting

With retrievers it is important to assess whether the dog perceives the retrieve as rewarding otherwise it will never be reinforcement for the hunting which precedes it.

To maintain motivation and speed the dog must have something to find. This is why it is so important to let the dog find the quarry and flush it in the first stages of learning.

HUNTING CRAFT

The dog's nose contains 220 million smell sensitive cells which makes them ultra efficient hunting machines. The dog will need to develop their searching skills for scent on the ground and in the air.

GROUND SCENT

Ground scent for the purposes of our teaching is the scent that is retained by the soil or vegetation that game has been in contact with by

Running that way

Staying to feed

Defecating

Sleeping in the afternoon sun

Rioja tasting the air

Ground scent gives an indication that the game is in the "proximity" but will not always mean that it is there now.

AIR SCENT

Air scent comes from the body of the game and rises in wafts of small particles, which is then carried and dispersed on the wind. This scent will indicate where the game is now.

It is important to use both scenting abilities for all the breeds of dog to broaden their reading capacity in the field. They are intrinsically linked and enhance the dog's hunting skills.

left: ground scenting

right: air scenting

FLUSHING DOGS

The flushing dogs, spaniels, mainly rely on ground scenting when hunting. This has been developed so they can work well as a team with the gun. They will work across the wind to quarter the beat at a close distance, around 3-5m, holding their head low to locate the scent. This distance is important and specified because it is based on half the average range of the shotgun. When the ground scent is located they will then run around busily until the game is flushed. If the working distance were any greater the success of the gun would be reduced. The flushing dogs are not expected to stop still in acknowledgement of the game, just continue to flush and re-hunt.

The flushing dogs need the skill to use the air scent initially and then make the transition to the ground scent to locate the quarry so as not to run over it.

THE HUNT POINT RETRIEVER (HPR)

The HPRs will use the air scent to locate their quarry when hunting, they will carry their heads at about shoulder height, dipping or lowering as they 'taste' the air or the conditions change. Their beat is far greater than that of the flushing dogs simply because of the development of the 'pointing' behaviour. This is the ability to remain still on the location of the game which gives the guns time to position themselves close enough in order to be able to make a successful shot.

The HPR's need to develop the skill of identifying the ground scent reading its message and then moving back to the air scent to firm the location and 'point'.

THE RETRIEVER

The Retrievers will need to use the air scent to locate a hidden bird or a bird that has dropped out of sight, moving to ground scent for locating a running bird that has been winged but not killed outright.

HUNTING WITH THE DOG

For hunting you will be teaching the dog four things

1. To thoroughly search a pattern

2. To identify the game from amongst the scents of other birds and animals.

3. To reject the scents of other similar birds and animals.

4. To identify where game has been and where game is by scenting either the air or the ground.

Most communication with dogs or by dogs is through their body language. By concentrating on using our own body language we have a very effective and appropriate means of communication.

In order for them to be successful when out hunting the group responds to slight changes in body language from each other. If the group leader at the time decides on a particular direction and sets off with purpose then the rest are drawn to follow. This effective strategy can be employed by us when managing our own dogs in the field.

When out walking (relaxed hunting) with my own four dogs, I very rarely go the same way or start and finish in the same place. I randomly change the direction of the walk (hunt) and draw the group with me. This is a continuous, low level training situation that tunes the dog into my body language. Most dogs do not like to lose sight of the main body of the hunt, and will learn to search and observe the behaviour of the rest of the group. If the rabbit poo or pheasant scent becomes over interesting then I will go off with purpose in search of something better, and have even been know to find my own, better poo. Very shortly all four will be in close proximity checking out what I have found. These are all variations on the **CATCH UP GAME** Recipe 30 *page 96*. They are developed further in the **RECALL TRAINING** *page 30 & 34.*

It is the managed movement with direction and purpose that indicates to the dogs that this the the the area to search and hunt. You can plan to demonstrate this by starting on fairly "dry" ground and moving towards the areas you know game like to collect. A youngster will soon begin to believe you have the same, but superior, hunting abilities and are a successful finder. Every reason to follow your lead.

Matching the dog's own behaviours of stalking, turning left and right and examining things closely. Minor changes in our own bodies give clear cues to the dog. For example leaning forward to go, leaning back to slow or stop, to the left or right to change direction.

Teaching the dogs to follow the scent route by using the changes in body language is in effect a simulated form of hunting. Using this body language consistently and appropriately with dogs teaches them that certain signals and cues relate to behaviours, for example the use of walking to the left or right when first teaching quartering. Making sure that they are always the same, a clear signal that the dog can see and appropriate for the task being requested. Any subtle changes in the delivery of these signals will affect the result of the response from the dog.

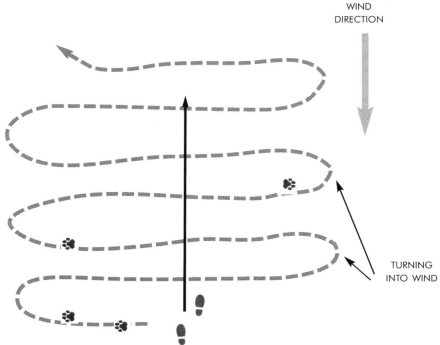

WIND
DIRECTION

TURNING
INTO WIND

QUARTERING

The true definition of quartering is where the dog runs to and fro whilst actually advancing in an up wind direction. It should have no relevance to your position. The dog should remain a reasonable distance in front of you, this will vary depending on the type of dog and be appropriate to the job they are doing. Pointers will be slightly further ahead than the spaniels. The pointing ability allows you to place the guns before the flush. The guns and you need to be closer when working with the spaniels and be ready for the flush. The dogs are

often expected to only quarter to the limit of a beat. A beat is the area specified either by the distance between each beater in a beating line or a defined area in rough shooting or tests and trials. The distance of a beat is greater for the pointing dogs than for the spaniels.

QUARTERING WITH THE WIND (above)

This is where the wind is blowing into your face and the dog will work from right to left across you into the wind. This is the best pattern to begin a young or inexperienced dog with. The dog will scent game ahead of himself and you.

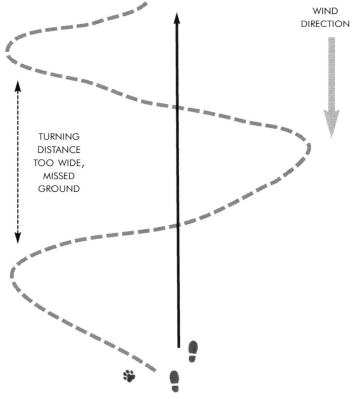

WIND
DIRECTION

TURNING
DISTANCE
TOO WIDE,
MISSED
GROUND

This is a general guide to this pattern and it is very unlikely that the dog will actually quarter as precise as this but the principle is that the dog turns into the wind and scents across always making the turn into the wind.

The distance the dog turns into the wind is an important factor. Too tight a turn without parallel runs will make the distance too great for the dog to scent correctly the result missed ground or ground that is covered twice.

QUARTERING WITH A CHEEK WIND *(above right)*

Here the dog works still at right angles with the wind but the wind is blowing onto your cheek instead of into your face. This is more difficult than quartering into the wind and will take some experience from the dog before beginning.

QUARTERING WITH A TAIL WIND *(right)*

Here you remain stationary at point A the dog quests out down wind as far as is appropriate for the task. The dog then quarters back into the wind towards you. The dog and you then move to point B where the quartering began and the dog is sent out again. This takes skill from the dog as well as experience as the dog must quest out in a straight line and not quarter, as there is a great chance that the dog will flush down wind.

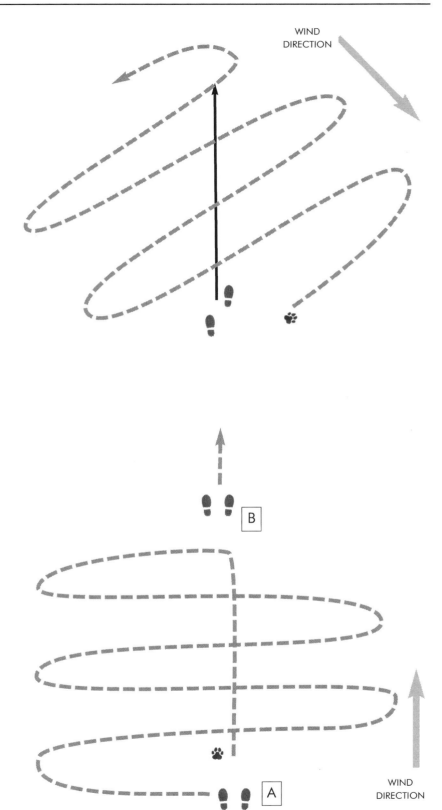

WIND
DIRECTION

B

A

WIND
DIRECTION

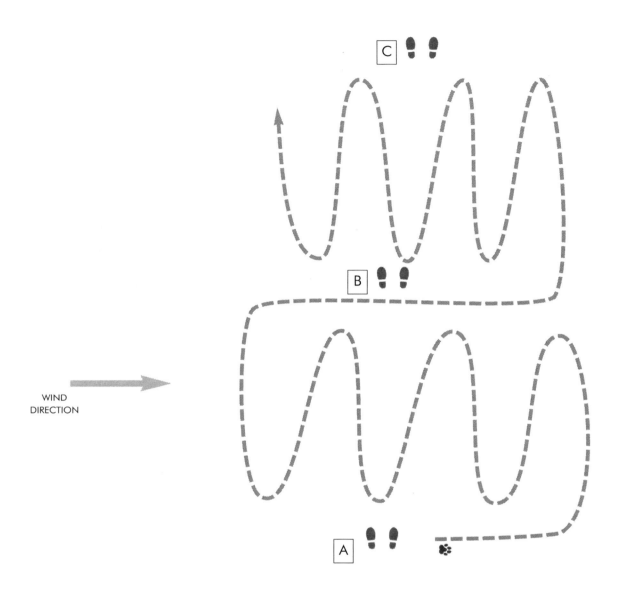

QUARTERING WITH A SIDE WIND

This is also a difficult quest, as the dog must be sent out down wind to the side of you. You then remain still at A, the dog quarters into the wind and passes across you. Once the appropriate beat distance has been covered you and the dog move to point B and the quest begins again.

The obvious point about all these different quartering patterns is that the dog always works into the wind irrespective of the location of you. They will never be this precise as the conditions always change, but the experienced dog will learn to adapt and change with the wind. The difficulties arise when teachers only define quartering as maintaining the to and fro pattern in front of them irrespective of the wind direction.

There is a disadvantage when working on organised shoots. The wind direction for the beaters will not be taken into consideration. The beat will be set up by the gamekeeper for the most effective way to flush the birds over the guns. The beating line is expected to move forward and push the birds on in that direction, and the experienced dog will often try to change its working pattern to the wind. Be aware what your dog is trying to respond to and the direction of the wind.

GENERAL SKILLS

Having already discussed selecting the right puppy or dog for the job and considered how learning takes place at crucial times during development it can be seen how important it is to introduce the dog to hunting, and the whole environment in which it will be expected to work, as early as possible. I take my litters of puppies out onto the farm with the older dogs letting them follow, experience the scents and open spaces, and absorb the art of hunting. This natural ability to hunt can show itself at six to eight weeks of age, where they already stalk the birds in the garden and respond to the scents. Early demonstration of the skills is not necessarily preferable, as many great dogs come into their skills later in puppyhood.

Hunting for the dog should begin as fun; the more intense training can be developed alongside and introduced gradually as the dog's experience and confidence grows. Hunting skill should be being built alongside the skills of control and retrieve.

At this early age it is difficult for them to get into too much trouble and they are still naturally under the influence and dependant upon their dam, this will easily be transferred to you as you begin to take on the role of providing them with a place of security from which they can build confidence, learn and turn to for trust and support. This is such an ideal time to start to slot into this partnership position with your dog.

RECIPE: 29

INTRODUCING THE DOG TO GAME

I take my puppies to a pen and allow them to move around inside taking in all the scent and sight of the birds while I fill up water bowls and feeders. I do this as a way of repaying the keeper for the courtesy of allowing me to teach my dog on his birds. Then I take the pup to areas outside where I know there will be birds and allow them to run about scenting and chasing and just having fun.

There is no need to introduce any control exercises at this early stage, all I am interested in doing is awakening the instinct to hunt, and I am looking for the natural abilities of the dog to come to the fore and allowing the dog to learn for itself. I can put the behaviour under stimulus control later on. A much easier way around than getting control too early and sacrificing the hunting ability.

An older more experienced dog will require the skill of the recall *(see **RECALL** page 30 & 34)* before teaching this skill. Or use a long line and manage the dog so that the birds are protected from being caught.

Begin by introducing the dog to game:

  ▶ Take the dog to an area where there are going to be lots of game and the scent will be very strong. If it is an organised shoot then make sure you have permission from the gamekeeper first. This should not be done for the first time on a shoot day.

  ▶ Let the dog run around and get the scent of the game for itself. If the dog comes across birds and they flush at this early stage it will do no harm but will help make the connection between the scents you will ask the dog to follow and the quarry.

  ▶ Always finish each session on a find.

RECIPE: 30

THE CATCH UP GAME

Puppies or young dogs will still be looking for guidance and check in with you. Take advantage of this and begin reinforcing it. This can be done by food reward and will help with later training when perhaps the stimulus may have become too much for the dog and they are unable to take food. By doing this early I have not yet had a dog that is unable to eat when training in the field.

You are teaching the dog:

▶ To always be aware of you in relation to where it is and what it is doing.

This game will begin to develop a relationship between you and your dog. It will also develop the skill of the dog to be able to keep on eye on you. This I refer to as 'checking in', a skill the experienced dog should have whilst working. If you change direction the dog should be aware and respond.

1. Take a bag of treats, your dog and yourself outside into the field.

2. Click and reward the dog for being with you.

3. Walk away with purpose in one direction; click the dog for catching up with you.

4. Repeat this several times changing direction each time.

5. Change the timing of the click so that you mark when the dog begins to follow you, before it has caught up with you. Reward when the dog reaches you.

6. Then change the time of the click to mark when the dog acknowledges you have changed direction and begins to move in your direction. Reward when the dog reaches you.

7. Change the reinforcement for the behaviour from the food to sending the dog off from you again.

8. Increase the criteria and distance from you, marking the acknowledgement behaviour whenever you make a directional change, stop or move off.

RECIPE: 31

EXPERIENCING THE ENVIRONMENT

This is especially beneficial for the puppy when it is still able to absorb information before having to actively participate in the learning.

1. Observe your dog before you go and note when they are relaxed.

2. Take your dog to the edge of the shoot on a driven day; let them experience all the noise, activity and scents that are taking place.

3. Make sure that you manage the situation and keep far enough away to ensure that the levels of stress are not too great for the dog. A good measure of this is when the dog refuses to take the food or play. Withdraw.

4. Play with the dog on the outskirts of the wood or drive, feed the dog treats and click it for the interaction with you whilst in this environment.

5. Play the **CATCH UP GAME** Recipe 30 while you are there.

RECIPE: 32

WING HUNTING GAME

If you are not fortunate enough to have access to live game to help develop and awaken the hunting instinct early on, then use a wing to the same effect. Here you are awakening the natural instinct in the dog to hunt.

Obtain a wing from a bird such as partridge or pheasant and attach it by string or line to a stick or pole. I use a bamboo cane from the garden. A fishing rod is very good for this as you can use the reel to move the wing quickly while not being too close to the dog. Not being a 'fishing person' myself the acquisition of a rod has to date eluded me.

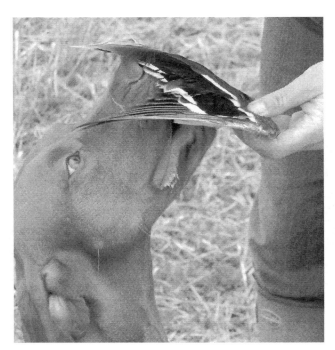

1.   Let the dog smell the wing, brush it gentle across their nose arousing interest.

2.   Then drag the wing along the ground let the dog follow and try to catch it, when they pounce launch the wing into the air.

3.   Treat this as a game. It doesn't matter if the dog catches the wing. At this stage it will only encourage them to work harder to get to it. This will improve their hunting skill.

4.   Repeat this frequently but only for about 5 minutes at a time. You want to maintain interest and build motivation but not tire the dog.

If you have difficulty getting hold of a wing, then use the fur off a toy or a piece of plastic bag, anything

TIP

The fleshy part of the wing can become a bit rancid after a while so I leave it outside to become fly blown first, letting the maggots eat the flesh from the top. Then I shake them out, give it a rinse under the tap and it is ready to use. The wing will last a long time and maintain its shape.

that arouses interest for the dog. Obviously the real thing is best as it generates a small amount of scent at the same time.

TROUBLE SHOOTING

Introducing stimulus control at this stage could be the cause of 'stickiness' in the pointing dogs or 'blinking'. Stickiness is where the pointing dog fails to move forward with the handler to flush the birds. Blinking is where the hunting dog locates the game but fails to acknowledge it either by flushing, pointing or working up to the game. Often turning away just before.

Take your time during this lesson; there will be plenty of time later to introduce the control behaviours.

You can begin teaching these separately away from the hunting games.

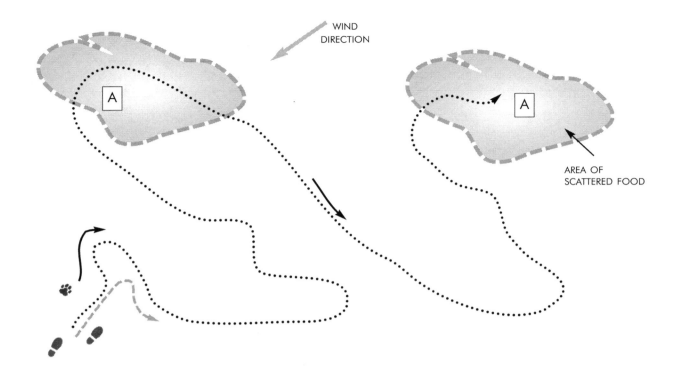

WIND
DIRECTION

A

A

AREA OF
SCATTERED FOOD

RECIPE: 33

HUNTING 'GO FIND'

Here you will be developing the dog's skill

▶ To set off from you on cue using their noses to scent

▶ To begin working an area to locate the reward

It is very important when using the click to mark behaviours, such as hunting, that your dog is already able to work through it. This is where the dog can be clicked for the behaviour, but the dog does not stop but continues on working for rewards. There are some excellent more suitable exercises in both the Novice and Intermediate books in the Clicker Trainers Series by Kay Laurence, that will help you develop this skill for your dog before you begin working on these more complex recipes.

1. Throw pieces of food over a wide area possibly in your back garden or an enclosed field or paddock

2. Encourage the dog to start to hunt for these pieces of food on the cue 'Go Find'

3. Begin clicking the dog for actually finding the food. Point A on the diagram.

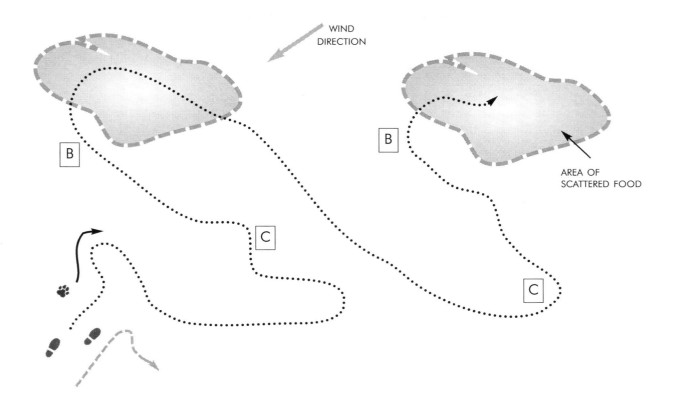

4. Change the timing of the click to mark when the dog is actually about to find the food, "on the strike" and let the dog self reward on the actual find. Point B on the diagram.

5. Then change the time of the click to mark the behaviour when the dog is actually hunting with its nose - scenting to locate the food. Point C on the diagram.

Engage in this with the dog. This will begin to develop the quartering pattern and introduce changes in direction for the dog, mimicking your own change in direction. Go with the dog on the hunt for the food, be close by when the dog makes the find. This will also help to develop the partnership between you and the dog whilst hunting.

Go in the direction where you know the food will be found and click the dog for following that direction. The dog will soon begin to realise that you are assisting with the finding of food rather than being incidental to the whole hunt.

Take this opportunity to click hunting together and very quickly the behaviour of scent/hunting will become self-rewarding.

If you are concerned about your dog's weight then use their meal to teach the hunt and set aside a couple of days a week to work on this. Doing this for every meal especially with puppies or young dogs may be detrimental to their growth and development as the effort expended to find their food would be far too much.

USING THE WIND

Introduce and use the wind to benefit the hunting for the food. Begin with working the dog into the wind. This is the easiest way for an inexperienced dog to learn. The wind should be blowing into the face of the dog. The dog will naturally work across this wind to search for the scent. This is often referred to as heading into the wind. Carry out all your early hunt training into the wind and this will develop confidence in the dog.

RECIPE: 34

HUNTING SPECIFICALLY PLACED FOOD

Teach the dog the skill of working across (cheek) the wind to help it locate the game. Quartering is the most efficient use of energy in relation to reading all the available scents in a specific area. Some dogs if left to their own devices, can end up going around in circles, covering the same ground and air many times.

All dogs need to develop their scenting abilities and build confidence. It will develop confidence in the retriever to use its nose and provide a sound base on which to develop quartering skill for spaniels and pointers.

You will be teaching the dog to:

▶   thoroughly search a pattern to locate

▶   identify the direction of the wind

▶   use the wind to locate

▶   locate using both air and ground scent

1. Place a piece of good smelly food in a specific location that you can relocate when returning with the dog. Make sure you have placed the food so the dog can work into the wind to locate it. (*See page 104 for marking specific locations*)

2. Send the dog out using your find cue.

3. Go with the dog at this stage but begin to move across the wind. Encouraging the dog to move across the wind with you.

4.   Click the dog for actively searching for the food.

This point of click is difficult to define, as each dog will hunt slightly differently. For my dogs it is when they are actually working with the wind, they have purpose in their movements, their heads are held at shoulder level or slightly lower, sometimes they raise or drop their noses tasting the air, mouths will be closed for tasting and this will depend on the quality of the conditions, tails are wagging. If you have spent time working through the previous two Recipes you will know what to be looking for at this point.

If you are unsure, look for the point when the dog suddenly locks onto the location of the food by scent. This is known as "acknowledging the scent", or a "strike". Begin by clicking this point then change the timing of the click to mark the scenting behaviour that comes before.

At this point the dog should be reinforced for the click by the continuing scenting and location of the food and will not break off to return to you for reward.

RECIPE: 35

USE COLD GAME OR SCENTED DUMMY

This recipe should only be used occasionally and the majority of the scent training should be done with food, and live and/or caged game. Cold game is game that has been shot and allowed to go cold before its introduction to the dog. This can be stored in the freezer for training purposes and allowed to thaw naturally before use.

At this stage it is important to continue to develop the retrieve skill separately following the recipes in the retrieve chapter. Both behaviours will then become very strong and self-rewarding individually. Using this recipe too much may reduce the quality of either the retrieve or the hunt depending on which your dog finds the most rewarding. You should be aiming to build a sound balance between the two skills.

You will be teaching the dog all the elements of the previous recipe plus the skill to

▶   identify the scent with the game

▶   identify the scent with the location of the game

1.   Place out cold game or a scented dummy in place of the food. Make sure you have chosen the location and memorised the line of sight.

2.   Send the dog out using your find cue.

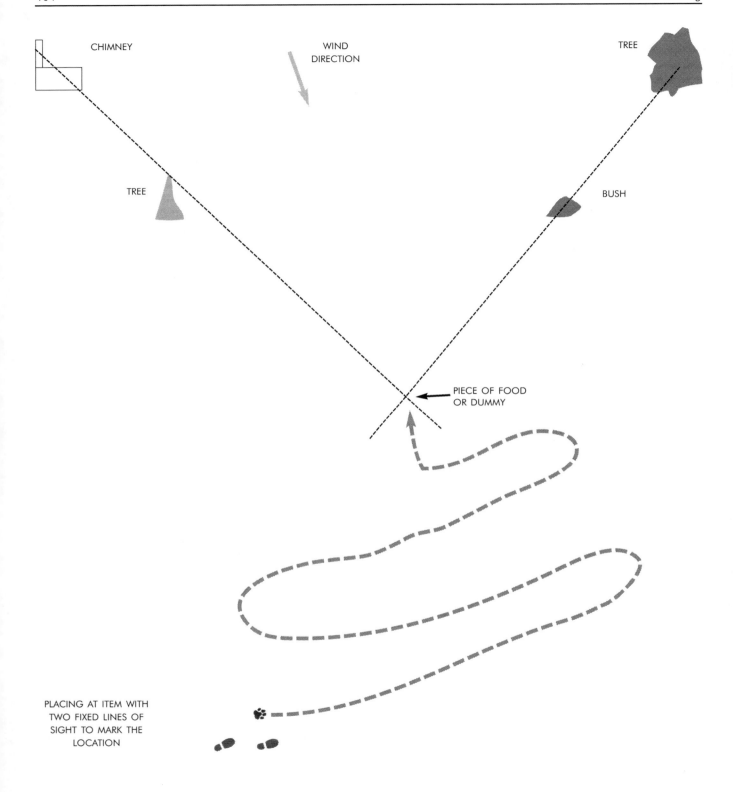

CHIMNEY

WIND
DIRECTION

TREE

TREE

BUSH

PIECE OF FOOD
OR DUMMY

PLACING AT ITEM WITH
TWO FIXED LINES OF
SIGHT TO MARK THE
LOCATION

FIXING A LOCATION FOR SCENT TRAINING

When you are setting out food and game it is important you know the exact location. Firstly, to assist the dog when training and secondly, if the dog is not experienced enough to find the game, it becomes extremely expensive to keep replacing them.

1. Establish where the wind is coming from then decide where you are going to place your food, or game.

2. Then look for two fixed points to the left and right. Pick fixed items such as trees, fence posts, telegraph poles, pylons, chimneys in the distance.

3. Then place the food or game at a location where straight lines from these fixed points cross. You will then be able to use them to relocate the article. (See diagram opposite). This will also be useful when you are placing your game or dummies for retrieve.

---

3. Go with the dog at this stage but begin to move across the wind. Encouraging the dog to move across the wind with you.

4. Click the dog for actively searching for the game or dummy.

Remember you are working on developing the skill of hunting and not retrieve. Continue to click for the active scenting from the dog, if the dog chooses to pick up the game or dummy then that's fine as is the choice not too.

RECIPE: 36

CONNECTING SCENT AND LOCATION OF GAME

To develop the dog's natural abilities and to make that important connection between scenting the game and the game itself is to use the real thing. This can be done without access to shoots or pens.

Here the dog is developing the skill

▶   To identify the scent of the game

▶   To identify the scent with the location of the game

USING PIGEONS

This is suitable for all dogs.

1.   Take a pigeon that can fly well. Hold it in your hands and let the dog sniff and nuzzle the bird.

2.   Let the bird go so it flies off and allow the dog to follow it.

3.   Repeat this 2 or 3 times and the connection will begin to be made.

USING BOB WHITE QUAIL

▶   The disadvantage of laying birds or dummies yourself, is the ground trail left by your footprints. The inexperienced dog can begin to search for your track and not the birds.

▶   Bob White Quail can be placed out once and then as they are flushed they will resettle in a new location not to far away that is completely free of your scent. You can mark the location of their settle and work the dog to this location.

▶   They can also be used later to refine the foundation behaviours and build stimulus control.

DIZZYING

You will need to learn the skill of 'dizzying'. I suggest you do this independently from the exercise with the dog. Dizzied birds are best used for teaching the pointing dogs.

1.   Change the pigeon for Bob White Quail.

2.   Place the head of the bird under its wing.

3.   Rock the bird to and fro gently.

4.   Place the bird down gently on the floor. If it remains still you have been successful. Leave it for a couple of minutes then gently nudge it out of the trance. The bird should get up and fly off.

Perfect this skill before introducing the dog to the exercise. You will also need a long stick to nudge the bird without getting too close when working with the dog. The priority here is the well being of the bird.

Using dizzied birds is especially beneficial for teaching the pointing & setting dogs. The recipe needs adaptation for use with the flushing dogs:

1. Place the dizzied bird out following the steps in fixing the location.

2. Begin to work the dog up to the bird using the skill developed in Recipe 34 & 35. 7Put the dog on a line so that you can manage the approach to the bird by the dog. A dizzied bird will not be able to escape and you are responsible for its safety.

3. When the dog "winds" the bird, click, and reward by allowing the dog to continue working. "Winding" the bird is when the dog locates it by scent not having been aware of its location before.

4. When the dog points the bird click and then you use your 'steady' cue and then nudge the bird out of the trance and allow it to fly off noting where it drops.

5. The puppy or young dog should be allowed to chase the bird at this stage; this will be the reward for the hunt and can be developed later into the flush on cue. The drop to flush in the foundation behaviours is taught separately from this exercise, then adapted to introduce stimulus control.

6. The older dog should be managed on a line or have the lead slipped on just prior to the flush. The chase must be prevented and the dog unable to catch the bird.

For the safety of the bird use a light weight long line on the dog, especially for the older dog, only use the line to prevent the possibility of the dog grabbing the quail or to control the amount of chasing.

Vary the use of the stick, as the movement of the stick to flush the dizzied bird can become the cue for the flush that the dog can easily anticipate and may try to run forward to pre-empt you.

DIZZIED BIRDS FOR FLUSHING DOGS

Here you will be developing the dog's skill

▶ To acknowledge the game

▶ Move onto the flush

Work through steps to dizzy the bird and place it out then

1. Managing the dog using a lead or line and approach the dizzied bird, nudge it fly off.

2. Make sure the dog watches the flush and where it settles

3. Work the dog up to the point where the bird settled looking for the acknowledgement in the dog of the bird's location.

4. Click the acknowledgement of the bird just prior to the flush. The dog should be allowed to follow through the flush. The older dog should be managed with the line.

5. The dog can flush at this stage as the bird will no longer be dizzied and be ready to fly.

SPECIALISED SKILLS

Remember that this is a chain built up from several individual skills and behaviours. When moving onto teaching the following recipes keep them separate until you have developed your foundation and control skills in parallel.

Each of these skills must be strong and flexible before you put them together in the chain or even merge with each other.

A CAUTIONARY NOTE

Be careful not to over use placed dummies, game and 'tame' game. Keep a balance with wild game. Dummies and game will have your scent on them, or scent connected with home.

Your exceptionally skilled gundog can distinguish between familiar training game and non-familiar wild game and they can inadvertently ignore wild game as not part of their training pattern. You will need to balance out the two, 'dogging in' is an excellent way of doing this and is covered in Chapter 6, Ready for the Shoot *page 147*

RECIPE: 37

USING CAGED BIRDS AND QUARTERING

You will be teaching the dog all the elements of the previous recipes plus:

▶ identifying the scent with the game

▶ identifying the scent with the location of the game

▶ thoroughly search a pattern to locate

▶ identifying the direction of the wind

▶ using the wind to locate

▶ locate using both air and ground scent

1. Place out the caged bird.

2. Send the dog out using your 'find' cue.

3. Go with the dog at this stage but begin to move across the wind. Encouraging the dog to move across the wind with you.

4. Click the dog for actively searching for the bird.

5. Refine your movement across the wind to the quartering pattern.

6. Click the dog for turning with you and continuing across the wind, here the continued hunt is the reward.

Refine the behaviour further by changing of the timing of the click:

Begin by clicking the turns

Change to clicking as the dog crosses in front of you and gradually reduce the amount of quartering you are doing

Allow the dog to develop the behaviour clicking the correct decision when to turn

Attach your whistle cue to the turn

NOTE

Allow the dog to work and develop its own quartering pattern with the wind. It will not match the perfect pattern in the diagrams as there will be many more external factors that will influence how the dog moves, such as wind speed, local gusting, natural obstacles, and the fact that at the dog's nose height the wind may well be moving differently than at our level.

The natural scenting ability of your dog will affect the amount of distance between the quartering lines and the speed at which the dog moves. The better your dog's natural ability is the more distance there will be and the faster the dog will go.

Attach your whistle cue to the turns. Use the cue to turn the dog only if they range too far out on the beat, otherwise leave the dog to quarter naturally. If you cue the dog to make every turn the dog will not learn the skill of when to turn in response to the scent and will range on until cued by you.

RECIPE: 38

STRENGTHENING THE POINT FOR POINTING DOGS USING THE WING

This follows on from **WING HUNTING GAME** (Recipe 32 *page 98)* used to awaken the hunting instinct in the dog. Again using the wing on the end of the pole or fishing rod. This is a game and there is no need to introduce any stimulus control at this stage. The dog is learning by trial and error. You are setting up a scenario as close to the real thing as possible. I use this with my puppies and young dogs.

You will be teaching the dog to:

▶ Develop the pointing behaviour

▶ Build duration

1. Take the wing and drag it along the floor encouraging the dog to follow and chase.

2. As the dog is about to catch the wing, fling it up into the air simulating the take off of a real game bird.

3. As the dog gets tired it will try to change tactics in order to catch the wing. We are looking for the dog experimenting with other behaviours.

4. If the dog begins to stalk, keep moving the wing along on the floor.

5. When the dog becomes still, click and reward by keeping the wing still. If the dog runs in to catch the wing launch it in the air just as the bird would do.

6. Introduce the 'steady' cue.

7. Change the timing of the click to build duration.

Each time the dog is still, the wing remains still on the floor and the dog is clicked, each time the dog runs in to catch it the wing flies out of reach. The behaviour that is reinforced the most is the stillness developing into the natural point.

When the dog is still (juvenile pointing) it is using its eyes not scent, stillness is stimulated by a visual cue. The connection must be made between point (visual cue) and the point (scent cue of the bird) as soon as possible. Following **HUNTING "GO FIND"** Recipe 33 *page 100* and **USING CAGED BIRDS AND QUARTERING** Recipe 37 *page 108* will maintain the balance.

RECIPE: 39

STRENGTHENING THE POINT FOR POINTING DOGS USING A CAGED BIRD

1. Catch a bird and place it in the release cage.

2. Take the bird out to a suitable location. Hide it in the undergrowth or hedge or behind a fence using the obstacle to obscure it from view and protect it from the over enthusiastic approach of the dog.

3. Before setting out, plan your approach. Take note of the wind direction and avoid tracking into the wind to the location.

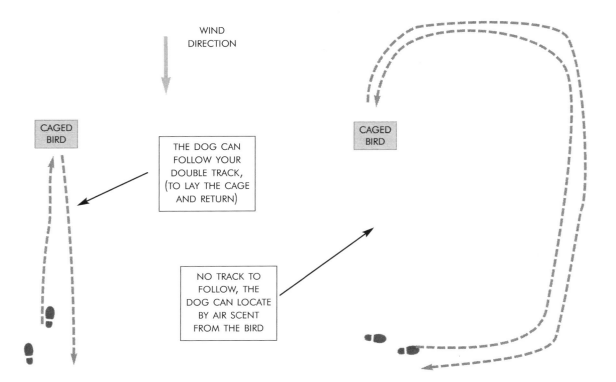

WIND DIRECTION

CAGED BIRD

CAGED BIRD

THE DOG CAN FOLLOW YOUR DOUBLE TRACK, (TO LAY THE CAGE AND RETURN)

NO TRACK TO FOLLOW, THE DOG CAN LOCATE BY AIR SCENT FROM THE BIRD

4. Set off your dog using your *'Go Find'* cue and work with the dog up to the caged bird.

5. When the dog becomes still on the scent of the bird click, and let the dog reward will oodles of scent wafting up from the bird. Begin to anticipate the point of stillness and introduce your 'steady' cue.

6. You should be with the dog at this point and remain quite still with the dog. Both you and the dog are pointing the bird together and working as a partnership.

7. Build duration into this behaviour by withholding the click slightly longer each time. This scenting will begin to then be paired with the cue for 'steady' making a self-rewarding behaviour.

RECIPE: 40

FLUSHING ON CUE

This is a skill required for the HPR's. Whilst holding the point for the guns to take up position, the dog will need to know when to end the point and move forward for the flush.

If the game flushes while the positions are being taken up, but the dog has not moved, it is likely that the noise spooked the game or the wind changed. Game has hazard avoidance behaviour and this will sometimes kick in taking the form of flight.

You will be developing the dog's skill to

▶   Hold the point steady

▶   Move forward only cue

Begin by teaching the dog the skill to move forward on cue by following Recipe 28 Walking Free *page 83*. You are beginning to build a chain of behaviours that begins with locating, followed by the point, followed by the flush and ending on the drop. You can adapt this recipe for use with the wing, caged game in a remote release cage, or wild game.

1. Work the dog up to the point, cue 'get on', click as the dog moves forward, lift the wing in simulated flush, release the birds, or watch the wild game flush. Let the flush reinforce the moving forward.

2. If the dog moves forward on the wing or caged birds before the cue is given, then you need to go back to increasing the steadiness on point and the behaviour of only moving forward on cue.

4.   If the dog moves forward on wild game but there is no flush, the dog may have been reacting to the change in scent as the game has run on. Click the dog for this decision and reinforce by allowing the dog to continue to work up to the game again, and begin again.

     If the dog moves in to a flush before the cue is given then the same applies as for the wing or caged birds. You must be there with the dog at the point stage in the chain and cue 'steady'. This steady cue should by now be paired with the glorious intake of strong fresh scent and as such be self-rewarding for the dog.

5.   If necessary have the dog on a line to manage the situation or slip the lead just before cueing the dog but take care as these then become additional cues which attach themselves to the situation and behaviour.

RECIPE: 41

THE DROP TO FLUSH HPR'S AND FLUSHING DOG'S

This is the final stage in the flushing chain. At this point you will have established your drop behaviour to cue separately following **DROP** Recipe 11 *page 45.*

You should have taught your dog the skill of being able take on a new cue. If not then I would suggest that you teach this skill following some of the recipes in the Foundation Book of the Clicker Trainers Series, *page 59* before continuing with this crucial part of the chain.

This skill is the final part of the chain and is the behaviour the chain should be driving towards. It needs to be taught out of the chain until robust. This place has to be the best place in the world as far as the dog is concerned and full of pleasure in itself. If you attach any anxiety or stress to it in the stages of teaching then you run the risk of devaluing it when it comes up against the actual flush or chase. You must be close to the dog and working in partnership to achieve the flush that, in the dog's mind, develops the idea this is the way to get the game killed, in this case shot, so that it can then be captured up.

If you do not have ready access to game birds then I would suggest that you establish the behaviour using the wing and caged birds. Be aware of the additional cues present from scent, the noise of the cage etc., and plan to make the transfer to wild game as soon as possible. This can still be done whilst working through the control exercises as it should be taught separately from the rest of the hunting chain and only brought together when all behaviours are in place.

You will be teaching the dog the skill to:

▶ Drop on the cue of the flushed game

1. Refresh the drop behaviour on your verbal cue. Use the wing on the pole and line, and lift the wing into the air as the new cue. Follow quickly with the verbal "drop" cue. Click for the drop, and reward. Look for drop on cue to be fluent and without hesitation.

2. Use the caged birds that you can then release remotely, but be aware the cages make a releasing noise that the dog can learn as the cue. You will be changing the cue not to the flush but to the noise, which will not be present on wild game.

3. Gradually fade the cue for drop as the dog anticipates the behaviour on the flush. Click for the anticipated behaviour.

4. Use another cued behaviour, such as heel, come, to release your dog from the drop. This interim behaviour will keep the end of the chain intact at this point and maintain the duration of the drop secure.

5. Take your dog to an area where you know there will be lots of game with a lead or line if necessary. Move into the game together, as they flush, cue the 'drop' and click and reward.

    Choose your reinforcement appropriate for your dog; it can be food, the flush, or approval from you. Consolidate this behaviour as much as you can. Gradually fade the verbal cue until the 'drop' occurs on the flush of the game. Always use an interim behaviour to end the duration of the drop.

    Attach a high level of reinforcement to it by calmly talking to the dog and gently stroking it behind the ears in a soothing way whilst in the drop. Avoid becoming animated or getting excited yourself, as this will only entice the dog to break the drop. This reinforcement has to outweigh the desire to chase.

It is highly likely that as soon as the dog is released from the drop it will want to rush to the place where the game was heading, by using the interim behaviour you can effectively manage what occurs next, take the dog away to another area and begin again, building up this 'idea' that the drop is the end and the flushed game is no longer of interest to the hunting party, there is more to be found or something else to be done.

VARIATIONS TO THIS RECIPE

If you have someone with a steady dog that already drops to flush then go out together, allow the handler to work their dog where there is game and you manage your dog.

When the experienced dog flushes you use this flush to teach your dog to drop. Dogs are very prone to "backing" as part of their cooperative instinct and you can use this trait.

Use the bolting rabbit as a starting point for the drop to flush on ground quarry. Set it up so that on release it is pulled directly away from you in front of the dog, and then change directions so it is moving away from all around the dog as rabbits do. Use the rabbit pen to set up a controlled environment and again flush the rabbits as you move through.

Remember you are teaching the skills required for dropping to flush.

RECIPE: 42

ESTABLISHING THE QUARTERING DISTANCE FOR BOTH FLUSHING DOGS AND HPR'S

As your behaviours become more reliable under test of increasing field stimuli, you can begin to introduce them to the hunting exercises. Begin by using the behaviours of stop and recall. Do not use your drop unless you are working on wild birds and have established the flush of these as your cue.

Set in your mind the distance that you require to work your dog ahead of you. Remember for flushing dogs it is about 5m or half the distance of the range of a shotgun. For HPR's it is the distance you and the guns can reasonably cover in a suitable time before the birds are alerted and flightier.

This will vary with the conditions of the terrain, wind and rain. In a good scenting day, when the wind is not too strong, the ground is dry and the air is warm. The scent from the birds will rise well and be carried on the wind. The dogs will pick this scent up very quickly and not have to range too far to be successful, they will scent the birds from a greater distance and be able to work up to them much easier.

If the weather is poor for scenting, perhaps there is a lot of moisture about on the ground and in the air, and it is cold. The bird's bodies will be cold and the moisture on them will trap the scent, preventing it from rising to be carried on any wind available. The moisture will also trap the scent and keep it close to the ground. Making air scenting very difficult.

A hard frost with no wind is also poor for scenting as the birds will be very cold and the scent will stay close to the ground. The dogs will have to range further to locate the scent and will be closer to the birds when they locate it.

1. Begin in an environment you can manage. Use a long line if needed but never to physically stop the dog. Allow the dog to reach the end of the line and walk up to them.

2. Use the principle of matching pace as discussed in **LOOSE LEAD WALKING** Recipe 25 *page 79.*

3. Every time the dog ranges too far the hunt stops. Use your 'stop' cue. Maintain your dog in position and walk up to them. Reinforce the stop. Begin again.

4. When the dog begins to anticipate the desired distance, click and reinforce by the continuing to hunt.

5. Vary this with recalling the dog to you. After recalling the dog, before casting off to hunt again change location.

TROUBLESHOOTING

It is not good to keep working your dog over 'old' ground or ground they have already covered. It will be instinctive for them to move directly up to the point that they were stopped and recalled from before they begin hunting again. The ground has been 'contaminated' with their scent and is no longer fresh. This will affect the information they can gain from any other scent present. For a young and inexperienced dog this is not good practice for teaching the scenting skills. An older more experienced dog will learn to read the information and pick out the important points from it.

Be aware when working with other dogs that your dog will naturally avoid working over ground where they have been, again, because of contamination of any scent present. When working in the beating line HPR's will naturally try to position themselves ahead of the other dogs so that they can work the air scent not yet contaminated.

You will have to make allowances and changes in your training programme to compensate for these external influencing factors. The flushing dogs will learn this skill as a form of patterning and it will be precise for them. The HPR's will need to be more flexible depending on the conditions. The game keeper will need to be convinced that your HPR is working the scent and steady on point, not "running in".

Stimulus control will be developing alongside this through the foundation behaviours and exercises for control. Use the long line or lead to manage the dog for the safety of the bird or to prevent the chase developing into a reinforcer. Remove the lead as soon as possible as it will become the cue for certain behaviours and contaminate others.

The dog that learns the skill of hunting when only wearing a long line and harness takes the cue to hunt from this equipment. When the line and harness are removed the dog is unable to hunt and has to learn all over again.

Take care not to yank the dog on a line or lead, as this will introduce stress or trauma to the behaviour. It may have a detrimental affect and even develop avoidance behaviour such as 'blinking'.

Let the dog reach the end and remain at this spot. Let the line be the guide to stop the dog and then walk up to the dog and begin again. It is your job as the teacher to manage and control the environment. When using a long line for management of the dog always put the dog in a harness this will make sure the dog is kept free from neck injury.

By allowing the dog to flush during early hunting exercises the dogs will develop an understanding of what will happen next and how close they need to approach to achieve this result. If one behaviour is given a high rate of reinforcement coupled with a high value reward it is likely to be repeated, and when compared with the behaviour that is not even acknowledged, this is the one that will fade.

The behaviours such as stickiness, blinking, back casting on scent, false pointing, boring into the wind and running in are all extreme ends of the hunting skills and have usually developed because stages have been jumped,or skills not developed correctly before moving on.

STICKINESS often results from never allowing the dog to flush or by introducing some trauma to the sequence at this point, such as yanking the dog on the line. Go back to the beginning and work through the exercises, think what behaviour you need from the dog, in this case moving forward to flush, go up to the dog, move forward fast and shape the dog to move with you. Follow the Recipe 40 **FLUSHING ON CUE** *page 112.*

RUNNING IN requires the sequence to be slowed down. Go back to controlling the learning environment and manage the dog on a line. Make sure you are close when the dog locates the game. You may need to go back to training some of the foundation behaviours such as the stop and drop.

Linking the hunting and the retrieve may result in the chain being lengthened. The dog may enjoy running more than the hunting; in this case the game is irrelevant so go back to increasing the value of scenting making sure that there is always a find. More work where there is lots of game.

BACK CASTING is where the dog turns down wind and begins to recover the ground that has already been worked. Lots more work with scent into the wind is required.

BORING into the wind is where the dog encounters large amounts of ground scent, stops quartering and follows this instead, at the end of the scent pool the dog begins to quarter again. Stop the dog and bring it back and begin again, mark the correct behaviour as the dog works through the scent pool quartering.

Allowing the dog to run on when tired, stressed or over excited will result in them panting. Once they start panting this will reduce their abilities to scent. When training a young dog avoid reaching this stage, put them on the lead and withdraw before you see these signs developing. If your dog begins to trip and stumble over obstacles or thick cover then they are already tired and you should withdraw.

WHERE TO NEXT?

Alongside teaching the dog these basic skills of hunting you will have been building on the control exercises and establishing the foundation behaviours. The next stage is to move onto wild game and build the chain, this is covered in the Chapter 6 Ready for the Shoot *page 147*. In order to move on to this next stage you must have in place some measure of stimulus control for your dog and the foundation behaviours.

5 **Retrieve Training**

For the majority of gundogs this is a collection of natural, raw skills that require some form of precision, generalisation and 'flair'.

The natural elements to look for in your dog are:

▶   The desire to grab things

▶   The proud strut

▶   The rubbing up against you while holding things seeking approval and reinforcement for the behaviour

▶   The general attitude of 'Mine'

The retrieve comes in the hunting chain towards the end and has been modified from the natural basic instincts of carry and consume. These skills were developed so that the pack could return to the den with food for the pups. You now wish to take this skill and develop it within the dog to retrieve specific game and dummies and return with them to you. The required game to be retrieved by the dog is also a resource of very high value. Take time over developing the retrieve skill.

I would expect the dog to take at least 6 months to reach the point of retrieving cold game confidently and reliably in a controlled environment, further work with warm game together with the control recipes is then required before taking out into the field environment that will then add the extra skill that only experience can give.

RECIPE: 43

RETRIEVE ASSESSMENT

Take the time to carry out a retrieve assessment on your dog. This will highlight the skills your dog already has in place and also the skills that need developing. It will also highlight if your dog is a reluctant retriever. From this assessment make a plan of which skills require shaping and which skills require breaking down into the behaviours and developing further.

1.   Take a selection of articles from the cuddly toys, ball, sock stuffed with socks to the dummy

2.   Throw them out in a scattered pattern

3.   Allow the dog to carry out its own idea of a 'retrieve'

4.   Take notes of your dogs skills including:

a.   The approach

b.   Pick up

c.   Way of carrying

d.   Selection of all or only certain types of articles

e.   The grab on pick up

f.   The desire to 'keep' or 'relinquish'

g.   The chase followed by brief interest only

h.   And if there is any interest in any article at all?

I include this last point because although for gundogs retrieve is assumed a natural instinctive behaviour it does not always manifest itself as such.

My 7-year-old bitch Kemble has excellent field skills and is a pleasure to watch while working the game but through an early inability to communicate she never made the retrieve connection. By relying on this natural ability if it fails to present itself as it did in this case it can be a major stumbling block. Kemble definitely did not find retrieving easy or self-rewarding. She was excellent at locating by scent but could not bring herself to pick up. Looking back this was evident right from the beginning. She never naturally carried anything - not even the softest of toys or the smelliest of socks unlike all the others. Through clicker training and micro shaping the behaviour in the smallest parts was I able to communicate to her what was required. As a result retrieving became rewarding and we both had a 'light bulb' moment. Then last season was a first for us both as a team, she hunted up, flushed a pheasant, I shot it and she retrieved it back.

HOW TO TEACH FROM THE PLAN

This will depend on the skill your dog displays as much as your skill as a teacher. As the teacher you have the following options

A.   Breaking it down into 'step by step' elements, each one taught separately, the pick up, the carry, the hold, the deliver, the run while carrying, the sit while carrying etc. This is the way forward for a dog like Kemble who has little or no inclination, mixed with 'puzzle solving' this will result in a very strong retrieve.

B. By 'shaping', taking the raw elements and developing them into the honed skills of the retriever. You will need good observation skills to pull out the exceptional parts of the raw retrieve, selectively click and shape the dog towards the final collection of behaviours.

C. By 'puzzle solving' setting the dog up in the learning process and allowing them to teach themselves the solutions. Where do you want this put? Oh you want it put in your hand! This way will result in a very strong retrieve with a dog that has the skill to self correct and adapt to any new situations. Sounds just like the perfect retriever exactly what we are looking for in the field! This process may take a while longer but the results will outweigh this extra effort.

Teach the retrieve independently from the hunting skill. When you have a reliable retrieve bring them together occasionally when training and if required in the field. If you follow the recipes then the game or dummy will automatically trigger (cue) the retrieve when found during hunting. Practising together or using the retrieve to trigger the hunting will reduce the quality in the two skills. This also applies to using the retrieve as the target for teaching the redirection. Imagine what impact this would have for a dog like Kemble if every hunt were followed by the retrieve as reinforcer.

THE SKILLS OF RETRIEVE

To sit holding the game/dummy waiting for the cue to give

Move into the sit whilst still holding

Move at speed and with purpose whilst holding

Negotiate obstacles whilst holding

Recognise the location for delivery

Pick up without hesitation

Pick up with a clean grip that will endure through the other tasks

Pick up without damaging

Carry without dropping or crushing it

Decide how best to pick up

Mark where the game/dummy has landed

Remain under control (sit) while the dummy is thrown

Remain under control (drop) while the game is shot after flush

Remain under control (sit) while the game is shot if picking up behind the guns

Remain under control (sit) while the game is shot if working next to the gun

You must teach each skill with care and precision to a high quality. Each step should be then put on cue and reliable before putting it in the chain. If you only teach your dog the skill to pick up one type of game bird or one dummy you may be conditioning them to retrieve only those items. This is often highlighted when unfamiliar birds such as woodcock or snipe are shot and the dog is unable to apply their learning to this new situation. You need to generalise as much as possible with the game or dummies you use when teaching. Your dog will then be able to apply this skill to the many different challenges that will present themselves when out in the field working. By doing this you will be building in flexibility right from the start.

RECIPE: 44

SIT AND MARK

Think of this skill in relation to the 'rabbit' you are teaching the dog to watch a rabbit hole. If the dog is too quick and jumps for the rabbit too early as it pops up out of the hole, the rabbit retreats and the dog will go hungry. In reality it is highly unlikely that the rabbit will come out of that hole again for a long time. We also know that if this is the case then the dog will continue to watch the hole for ever and a day and will return time after time just to check. So your dog will need to exercise self-control and wait for the rabbit to re-emerge and move away from the hole to be successful. This is an essential survival hunting skill.

This recipe will teach the dog the skills

- ▶ To focus and maintain concentration

- ▶ Keep their eye on game

- ▶ To maintain a high degree of self control in the presence of visual distractions

- ▶ To note the location

- ▶ To begin developing speedy movement from a stationary control

1. Begin by sitting on the floor, facing the dog. Put a piece of food on the floor between you, but keep your hand very close to the food. Wait, if the dog goes for the food place your hand quickly over it to prevent the dog from taking it. The dog will probably decide to try another tactic like in the wing game, if the dog backs off, or remains under control, click, pick up the food and toss it away for the dog to go and get.

   Note: the dog should never take the food from the floor where you placed it.

   At this point the dog has been rewarded for the tiny amount of self-control they exerted by NOT taking the food.

2. Extend this behaviour and skill in length of time. Make sure you only click when the dog is watching the piece of food and holding control. The position of the dog at this stage is irrelevant.

3. Continue to repeat until the dog is anticipating the behaviour and remains still on the placement and some duration of watching the food.

4. Once this behaviour is established and reliable add your 'mark' cue. This will then be used in the future to teach the dog to look in the correct direction for thrown dummies.

5. Vary it slightly from picking up the food and throwing it to flicking it away, you may have to encourage the dog to go for the flicked piece in the beginning as they may well be fixated still on the spot. This will develop a stronger fix on the 'rabbit'.

   If the dog looks away when they should be marking the rabbit then you steal the food and put it back in the pot. Hey? Lost rabbit.

6. Transfer this behaviour to when the dog is sitting at heel, begin by kneeling next to your dog and throw the food forward. Position yourself slightly behind the dog so your hand movement is not a distraction.

7. Your click needs to be for maintaining the 'sit' and looking at the piece of food at the same time. You can deliver the dog a piece from your pocket, and leave the marked piece on the floor for the next behaviour.

8. Become unpredictable in the delivery of the food reward so that you can anticipate the dog's anticipation. Vary by feeding the dog in the sit with additional food, collect yourself, and sending the dog to collect it.

9. Introduce your 'mark' cue before the throw of the next piece of food, click for the dog looking forward and maintaining the 'sit', keep varying the reward delivery.

10. Gradually move yourself into the standing position beside the dog.

11. Gradually increase the distance of the throw.

Teach this skill independently from the chain of retrieve behaviours and concentrate initially on using the food, otherwise you will likely build anticipation into the behaviour when using the dummy especially if your dog is a very strong retriever and self rewards on this behaviour. Again, maintain the element of unpredictability: not every dummy thrown means 'fetch', not every piece of food means "eat".

Adopt a particular body position when setting the dog up for the mark which will help distinguish it from the set off to hunt, for example, stand relaxed with your feet apart. This skill will be the basis for developing the seen and directed retrieves.

RECIPE: 45

MARKING FROM THE SHOT

You will also need to teach the dog the ability to 'mark' the dummy or game when shot, thrown or launched. This is a skill that should develop from the previous recipe. The game or dummy is not always going to land at the distance equal to your throwing ability. When launched from a dummy launcher the distance is far greater and often the dummy will land in cover and not be seen. Also the dog will need the skill to note the rise of the gun and to follow the direction of the shot in order to mark the falling bird and remain steady, not reacting to the sound.

The additional skills here are:

▶ The ability to watch the game and mark its drop point

▶ The ability to take direction from the start position

▶ The ability not to react to the sound of gunshot

1. Begin by asking someone to throw dummies for you, set the dog up, as you would for the mark, click the dog for watching the dummy fall.

    Change the timing of the click to develop which area is the weakest. If the dog misses the throw then wait for the dog to watch and click at this point. If the dog tends to miss the landing click when they watch it land.

    Build strength into the idea that the dog needs to keep an eye on the bird all the time if it is to be 'captured up'.

2. Anticipate anticipation with unpredictability: sometimes you collect the dummy, sometimes the other person collects it and unless you have completed the teaching of the retrieve chain keep it separate, but if you have; then begin to allow the dog to reinforce on the retrieve. By keeping this varied you will maintain the quality in the control, the mark and the retrieve chain.

2. Change to using a dummy launcher. Before you progress through this step you MUST first have introduced your dog to the sound of gunshot. Follow the recipes in the Foundation Training Chapter 2 *page 23*.

3. Begin by making sure that you and the dog are facing the same direction as the launched the dummy. This will develop the dog's ability to take note from your body language the direction in which to begin watching. Initially the dog will mark the point the dummy lands, but with repetition the dog will begin to watch your lift to fire the launcher and follow the path of the dummy as it travels. Change the timing of the click to match this.

DUMMY LANDING ZONE

BOTH HANDLER AND DOG ARE CORRECTLY FACING THE LANDING ZONE

DUMMY LANDING ZONE

DUMMY LANDING ZONE

DOG IS LINED UP INCORRECTLY

HANDLER IS LINED UP INCORRECTLY

4. We have now begun to make the connection between the change in body language and the lift in the launcher as the cue to mark, which equals: *'watch for the bird, keep watching it as it travels and take note of its landing point ready to capture'.*

It is important to maintain that the release to retrieve only takes place on the verbal cue from you. In order to achieve this always follow the unpredictability rules described earlier. Not every launch results in the retrieve. Anticipate, anticipation. We teach the dogs to puzzle solve and anticipation is good evidence of a bright dog working out what comes next. The noise of the launcher firing must never be the cue to retrieve.

The process is exactly the same when you introduce the gun. As the gun is lifted, click and reward, and cue the dog to mark for watching in the direction you and the gun are pointing. Gradually begin to change the criteria with the introduction of the noise of the shot, shot followed by thrown dummies, and lastly shot followed by game. (*See Chapter 6 'Ready for the Shoot', page 147*). This criteria jump should not be introduced before all the stages in the retrieve chain and the control exercises have been completed. The dog should also have been introduced to warm game in a controlled situation.

Remember you are developing the merged behaviours of control, sit and mark. Should any aspect begin to deteriorate then you need to drop back and re-build strength into the weaker area. It is a rare dog that has equal strength in all parts of the retrieve. If you skip a stage or especially let the controlled sit deteriorate you will be heading for disaster and the likely result will be a dog running in on the sound of shot.

The mark cue for the dog must equate to

► Maintain your position

► Watch the direction of travel

► Note the landing

► Wait until given the verbal cue to move

RECIPE: 46

COLLECTION AND DELIVERY

From experience of teaching dogs to retrieve by both shaping (from the raw skill) and completely breaking it down (for the dog with no raw skill), I believe that the dog that has learned and developed through self teaching and puzzle solving is the stronger. They have a sound understanding of what is required, and are able to transfer the skills to different game and situations with ease. Ultimately we try to set up learning situations that match the natural trial-and-error method of learning.

Having carried out your initial assessment on retrieve in Recipe 43 *page 120* you will be able to identify which type of object your raw retriever preferred. If they prefer the socks or cuddly toy then we will use this information to adapt our dummy to make it more attractive. With the puppies I allow them to carry about the socks and cuddly toys, then using this initial experience to make the transition to the dummy.

I often wonder why we use the dummy, it has no real link in shape or texture to the final game, but is useful for mimicking the weight. There are some new dummies on the market shaped like birds with wobbly heads designed to imitate the real thing. I have not used them yet but I can see the benefit to this shape design, especially when teaching the dog the skill of where to hold a bird.

If your dog choose the socks or cuddly toy then take the unwashed material and wrap it around the centre of the fi lb puppy dummy and stitch in place, or stuff the dummy inside the sock. If your dog was happy to pick up anything and everything from the pile then, if a puppy, begin with fi lb puppy dummy, or if an older dog then begin with the 1 lb dummy.

Find a container that the dummy will comfortably fit into, some ideas are a low-sided basket, washing up bowl, plastic box etc. Make sure the dog is happy with interacting with this before you start.

TIP

I have found when teaching retrieve with all my dogs that the food can be a stumbling block. I am unsure if it is the shape of the gundog's mouth or because of the material and shape of the dummy. The food sticks to the roof of the dog's mouth and they then use the dummy to get it off. This behaviour reduces naturally as the retrieve skill develops. To reduce it quicker I found using cheese cubes or polony sausage pieces instead of the flat thin pieces of meat worked better, also give them time to eat the food in between, this slows the process slightly but decreases any mouthing on the dummy.

The retrieve object can become a high value resource that triggers the 'parade' reflex or even the refusal to relinquish. Because of the importance we place on taking the game bird from the dog, it often triggers an anxiety in the teacher. When these two emotions are mixed together, stress, anxiety can build and contaminate the behaviour. By using the container at this early stage we remove any association that the dog is giving up something to you, and we can also strengthen the sense of working together, rather than in opposition, to help the dog solve the puzzle. View the container as the 'target' for the dummy that can then be faded, and replaced by hands. You are teaching the process of retrieve that the dogs are very good at learning.

Hey what a great end to a hard day when the dog collects all the game up and puts it in the bag itself! Putting the obvious practicalities aside a great party trick.

1.   Place the dummy in the container on the floor. As the dog looks inside, click and place the food in the container. A good position for you to be in while teaching this is sat in front of the dog with the container by your feet.

2.   If the dog is not curious let them see you take a piece of food and put it under the dummy click when the dog nudges the dummy to get the food.

Continue to pretend to place food under the dummy and click for the nudge with the nose to get it, drop the food in to the container.

3.   Take time with this criteria to consolidate the learning and wait for the anticipation as you place the container on the floor.

For the raw retriever these next criteria stages will develop quite quickly, but still make sure you consolidate each stage before moving on. It will be tempting to jump some stages but to gain the maximum understanding develop each stage slowly, take your time, remember you are developing a skill that you will want to use with a very high resource in a very stimulating environment, by investing time now you will ensure the dog understands what is required and help adapt easier to the environmental stimulus.

4.   Increase the criteria and look for more than a nudge - a mouth around the dummy, click this as soon as it appears. Now click for nothing less. The lift is likely to develop at the same time, or fairly soon, so be prepared to time the click so that the dog releases the dummy back into the container.

    Reward with food to the container. Be selective and only click for the dog's mouth around the centre of the dummy; eliminate any pick-ups from the ends at this early stage.

5.   Only click if the dog is using its head and mouth, any introduction of feet should be shaped out at this stage.

6.   Begin some generalisation for the dog. Move the dummy in the basket, put it against the side so the dog has to move its head to pick it up or move around the container, balance it on its end so that you can completely eliminate the pick ups from the end. Take each criteria one at a time and consolidate the learning before moving on.

At this stage you have conditioned the dog that the dummy needs to be picked up around the middle and be in the container in order to get paid. In essence you are building the chain by putting together little pieces of a puzzle, the dog's task is to work out which piece of the puzzle belongs where.

We have built the picture in the dog's mind that the dummy belongs in the basket, this is what gets paid, so by making some slight changes to this we can develop it further. The next step is to give the dog the skill to return the dummy to the container.

7. Place the dummy outside the container, close by and at the same height. This is a difficult step for the dog. You will continue to pay when the dummy is in the container, and the food will still be delivered to the container. You will click for the skill of getting the dummy back into the container.

     This is teaching the dog the skill of picking up and lifting. An important skill for the field dog considering the weight of some game.

This is the difficult part for the dog, imagine having to pick up a pheasant with your mouth and then carry it while moving at speed and over obstacles. Picking it up and putting it down may be quite easy but it requires a different way of holding in order to be able to carry it and move with it. This is where the skill of lifting is so important. You will want the dog to be able to pick the game up in the carry grip right from the start. You will not want the dog to pick the bird up and then toss it about until it gets it in the right position to carry. You also do not want the dog to start picking it up by the wings or head and carrying it along swinging in front of them. Take time here as the dog learns the skill of picking the dummy up and having to lift it high enough to go over the sides of the container, they will be self teaching the skill of carrying with a good head carriage.

RECIPE: 47

GENERALISE DUMMIES AND GAME

Choose a variety of different dummies at this stage to encourage the dog to develop the skill of picking up different weights, textures, scents and shapes. I follow on with the different dummy weights, the dummy covered with rabbit skin or wings, the parcel of wings and cold game.

Each object is designed to allow the dog to make the transition easier from something that bears no resemblance what so ever to game to what game will actually feel like to pick up. At this stage remove the wings from the cold game initially so that the dog can learn the skill of picking the bird up around the middle without the added distraction of flapping wings. If you are teaching a puppy you will need to take time with the weighted dummies until the teeth have developed fully and match the weight appropriately to the growth. If your dog is finding the transition difficult sometimes wrapping the bird up in a stocking makes it easier, this can then be gradually faded as the dog becomes accustomed to the texture.

RECIPE: 48

ADDING THE CUES

In essence your dog has now learned a retrieve, it may only be a very short distance and to a target container, but every skill they need they have taught themselves through this process. Your next task is to add cues, and to change the criteria to include distance, obstacles and speed. You should also only be selecting for your top quality pick up.

1. Having generalised through the different dummies and game, go back to your standard 1lb dummy for older dogs or fi lb dummy for the puppies.

   Begin at the last stage where the dog was competent at putting the article from the floor into the container. Selectively click for only your top quality pick up. There should be no adjusting of the dummy once it is in the dog's mouth, or any mouthing. This is the point to eliminate these. The pick up should be clean in the centre of the dummy.

2. Add your cues; give the cue just as you anticipate the behaviour will occur. There are two behaviours, the 'fetch' is the pick up and the 'give' is for the drop into the container.

3. Gradually get your dog used to having your hand close to the dummy as they pick it up.

RECIPE: 49

MORE SHAPING ON THE PICK-UP

You will now take the pick up out of the retrieve chain and begin shaping it until it is very strong, accurate and top quality. Then it can be re-built back with the chain.

By doing this you can limit the number of behaviours offered and clearly see to click the desired result. This is the final stage to eliminate any mouthing or pick up difficulties that have developed.

Be extremely conscious of what you click for at this stage any doubt and it is best not to click. One miss timed click for the chomp on the dummy or the grab at the end and you will have to begin all over again or risk the chance of building it into your chain.

It is much easier to see exactly what the dog is doing as it approaches you than it is at a distance. Imagine throwing the dummy out and then trying to get yourself into a position to see what the dog's mouth is doing on the grip in order to be able to selectively click to eliminate the mouthing. I have tried this and due to the difficulty in seeing, the number of clicks for what I could see became very low. The reinforcement rate for teaching this skill was very poor and did nothing to improve the behaviour I wanted. By turning it around and teaching it facing the dog, I had a clear view and could easily select the behaviour I wanted, eliminating any mouthing much quicker. Additionally this paints the picture in the dog's mind at this stage that dummy and you belong together. Reinforcement happens when you are both in proximity, and this becomes the first response on pick up. Very useful to be able to highly reinforce this connection before the introduction of the high value warm game. No worries- retrieve becomes a breeze!

You are changing the dog's idea of 'capture the game' to 'capture the game and deliver it to you'. You are also consolidating the idea that you are a partnership and jointly involved in moving through the links of the hunting chain helping the dog understand that this is how things get carried back for consumption.

1. Hold your dummy just off the floor; make sure you hold it at the ends with both hands and never in the middle, click for the grip. Allow the dog to drop the dummy and feed to the floor. Watch the location of the clicker to the dog's ears when doing this exercise, if necessary dull your clicker with 'blue tack' or use a quieter type, or even place the clicker under your foot.

2. Increase the distance you throw the food away. Make sure the dog has to leave you to collect the food, then as the dog turns back to come towards you and the held out dummy, cue 'fetch'.

3. As the dog then opens its mouth on the approach to grip the dummy, click and throw the food behind and away from the dog. This is teaching the dog the skill of a good speedy approach on your cue. Generalise this around you and at different heights.

4. When this becomes fluent and the dog is moving in with good speed, change the timing of the click by withholding it for slightly longer, until the dog completes the grip.

   Slide the click further along the behaviour until the dog has a sound grip and holds the dummy stable in its mouth.

6. Remove your hand and click for the independent hold.

7. Re-introduce the dummy and container. Incorporate a run up to the dummy that should be located on the floor near to the container. Gradually increase this distance with the thrown reward.

RECIPE: 50

CHANGE TO HAND DELIVERY

You will be teaching the dog the skills of

▶   Delivering to you

▶   Accurately locating the delivery point

▶   Relinquishing on cue

You may find this easier if you sit on the floor next to the container.

1.   Place your hand over the container so as the dog drops the dummy it will land in your hand. Gradually fade away the container until it is replaced with just your hand. *Prior to this stage I will already have targeted the dogs chin to my hand (Recipe 7 page 38) which helps with the transfer as the dog is already used to lifting its head to locate your hand.*

2.   Gradually increase the criteria so the dog is running in from collecting the food picking up the dummy and lifts up its head to put it in your hand.

3.   Do this in small steps: start sitting on the floor, to a stool, then to a chair and finally to the stand.

4.   You will click for the placement of the dummy in your hand.

5.   Remember to be very selective with your click, avoid encouraging mouthing or repositioning of the dummy in the dog's mouth as it tries to locate your hand.

6.   Consolidate this so that you and the dog have hold of the dummy at the same time, then change the click timing, introduce a 'give' cue and click the dog for releasing on this cue only; not as it places the dummy in your hand.

This is an important skill to develop as sometimes the game may not be dead on retrieval, if this is the case the last thing you want is for the dog to release the game before you have hold of it and it runs or flies away. This is in effect your previous 'give' cue as the dummy was dropped into the container.

RECIPE: 51

WHICH WAY TO DELIVER?

It is at this point you will need to decide on selective cues for the dog to deliver the dummy under different circumstances.

The different circumstances are:

▶   picking up and sweeping through after a drive

▶   formally picking up behind a gun

▶   you are the gun and your dog will be retrieving for you

a.   If I am picking up and sweeping through after a big shoot it is likely that I will be moving around with the dogs as they search. I will not require the dog to sit to deliver each bird to me, I will expect hand delivery and send the dog off straight away to search again.

Here I will consolidate the hand signal cue developed above. The cue will be me standing with my right hand held out to take delivery. The hand is the cue to locate to not to release, the dog and I will hold at the same time and the dog will release on the verbal cue 'give'.

You have a powerful reinforcer to make use of: after delivery the dog is rewarded with more hunting. You need to watch that the hunting is not more reinforcing otherwise the dog may begin to drop the game before completing the retrieve chain. If so put in an interim behaviour such as 'wait' before sending the dog off again.

Thorn returning with a partridge - a good hold and good pace

b. If I am formally picking up behind a gun or shooting myself I will require the dog to sit in front following the retrieve.

Firstly, the dog should not be freely searching while the gun is still shooting unless sent for direct retrieves under certain circumstances, for example, the bird is hit but not dead and is likely to run. Etiquette dictates that it is your responsibility to secure all shot game.

Secondly, for practical reasons, usually if you are the gun your hands will be full with the gun and would have difficulty collecting a bird from the dog at the same time.

To develop this skill you will need to have already completed working through the sit in front from a recall *(Recipe 5 page 36)*. Begin by refreshing this with the dog.

1. Cue the dog to sit in front, whilst sitting offer the dummy with both hands and cue 'fetch'. Whilst the dog remains in the sit and holding the dummy take this opportunity to gently stroke the dog very calmly whilst resting their chin in your target hand.

   The dog should be relaxed and calm and quite at ease to place its chin in your hand. Remember your hand should not cue the dog to release this comes only on the 'give' cue. If the dog is releasing on your hand cue you need to go back and develop this further before continuing. Click and take the dummy.

The reinforcer for this retrieve is not going to be as great as previously discussed, as the dog will more than likely need to sit and wait to be sent for the next retrieve. So in this case we need to make the idea of being in this location, and position with the dummy a really great place to be and one full of reward. It needs to be calm and controlled.

2. Put this back into the chain of behaviours. Put the dummy by your feet, throw a piece of food away to get the dog to move away from you. As the dog turns back cue 'fetch' for the dummy and then cue the recall to sit in front.

   At this point you can click for any behaviour in the chain, but after the click, cue the next behaviour. If you click the fetch then cue the recall that will trigger the sit in front. Stroke the dog, put your hand on the dummy, cue the 'give' then feed the dog. Here you are attaching pleasure to the cue to recall, as such it will also begin to act as a reinforcer.

3. Increase criteria by placing the dummy further away, avoid throwing at this step, as you will be introducing stimulus in the form of prey that needs capturing. It is better to remain controlled, as the learning process is not yet complete.

4. Continue to build the distance and cue the dog for the present.

RECIPE: 52

THE COMPLETE CHAIN

Here you will be completing the chain by bringing the mark, fetch, return and deliver together. First you need to refresh the dog with the sit and mark for the dummy as in Recipe 44 *page 123*.

1. Begin to release the dog from the mark with the 'fetch' cue, make sure your dog does not anticipate this release, it is important that they do not go on sight of the dummy. Click for the mark and use the fetch cue to reinforce the control.

2. Vary the point of click to different points during the chain and use the following cue as the reinforcer. So if the mark is clicked the fetch cue reinforces, if the fetch is clicked the recall cue reinforces etc. Your dog should have developed the skill of working through the click if you have begun to develop the recipes in the other chapters but if not they may stop or drop the dummy, just cue the point in the chain at which they broke off and they will soon get the idea.

3. Begin to drop off your cues until you have the minimum amount. Start losing the last first.

4. You will always have environmental cues and object cues that will trigger the chain for the dog, the dummy will trigger the pick up and return.

5. Change criteria again, introducing all your different dummies, up to cold game.

    The criteria should be changed one step at a time so if you are changing weight then do not change texture to feather or fur at the same time. Begin with weight change in the dummy consolidate this, then go back to your original dummy and attach wings, then fur, then change weight again with these and finally the cold game.

    With the cold game begin with light birds first such as partridge, then move to the heavier, introduce rabbit before hare. Pigeons are not the best birds to use to introduce feather, as they are so soft just on touch the feathers can come out. Some dogs find of a mouth full of feathers an off putting experience and will drop the bird to get rid of them or bite harder to try and stop them coming out. These are birds that should be introduced in the final stages of consolidation and gener-alisation.

    Lastly introduce warm game. Choose an environment that you can manage with the least amount of stimulation. You want to avoid making the connection between this capture and stimulation. This will be your dog's most valued resource but treat it the same as all the other changes you have made.

6. Generalise further to teach the dog the skill of holding and carrying the dummy in any location during any activity, such as getting in the car etc.

Sitting	Standing	Running
Jumping up	Jumping down	Up & down stairs

All this practise will strengthen the dogs skills when out in the field. Your dog may need to retrieve from under the hedge, from on top of a hedge, through a hedge or in a hedge. The more practise off the field, the easier the skills can be applied to new situations in the field.

The skill of jumping while retrieving is covered in Recipe 56 *page 143*. For the safety and well being of the dog I teach the dog to jump as a skill on its own see Recipe 9 *page 42* in the Chapter Foundation Training.

Take your time, invest your energy into teaching and your dog will consider new game keenly and with interest. Creating opportunities for the dog to succeed and remove any anxiety or fear of failure from the challenge. If your dog is having difficulty in making a transition, for example from cold to warm game, then go back and work more with cold game, to build their confidence. Sometimes we need to be creative to make the steps of the transition easier for the dog to progress, and look for a way to make game change from cold, to slight warm, to warm, quite warm and then hot, rather than lead straight from cold to warm.

A CAUTIONARY NOTE

If you are using dummies and cold game and handling them you are transferring your scent to them. Through frequent use they become familiar, with mixtures of your scent, ground scent and the dog's own saliva. Gundogs in general are very good at transferring from one thing to the next and tend not to be particularly fussy about what they pick up.

But be conscious that on a shoot, your dog is not locating a familiar object, but a strange, sometimes novel game or dummy. Where possible plan to introduce the dog to unfamiliar objects throughout the training.

TROUBLESHOOTING

FAST OUT SLOW BACK

If your dog is faster on the run out and slow on the return then it is likely that the retrieve still presents the 'idea' to them of a 'capture' not a 'capture and deliver'. The collection of the game is giving them more reinforcement than the delivery to you. This needs to be re-balanced with high levels of reinforcement on arrival.

If your dog runs out but only walks back it may be because they have not learnt the skill of running while holding the dummy. Cue the dog to 'fetch' then run alongside the dog while it is holding the dummy, click for the running and holding and build on this skill. Attach a cue 'fast' and then use it to re build your chain.

SQUIRRELS

Take care if you intend your dog to retrieve such things as squirrels on a mixed bag day. Some keepers even encourage the shooting of squirrel as it is classified as a pest. The squirrel is a tenacious little devil and if not dead will deliver a nasty bite to your dog as they attempt to retrieve it. Either check first to make sure it is dead before sending your dog for the retrieve or leave it to the more experienced. I have seen young dogs traumatised by this experience that then causes immense damage to the retrieve. Even in a trial environment I would ask that the judge check if the squirrel was dead before sending one of my dogs, though these days this is less likely to occur.

RUNNING IN

'Running in' is where the dog runs to retrieve either on sight of the thrown dummy or at the sound of the gunshot. Anticipating the handler's cue. This is pertinent to all retrievers. This often results because no delay has been introduced following either the throw, or the sound of gunshot. There should always be a pause between the game landing, the dummy landing, or the fired shot before the dog is released on cue to 'fetch'. Anticipate anticipation, this is one situation when prevention is the far shorter route than a cure.

If your dog is breaking the mark then introduce an interim behaviour such as wait:

Sit Mark - Wait - Gunshot - Wait - Throw - Wait - Landing - Wait - Fetch

By clicking and rewarding ALL the wait behaviours in this sequence, you will re-balance the chain.

The wait cue can then be faded when the sequence has been re-established. Be creative and look for other behaviours that can follow the final wait, such as a down, walking away to heel, getting into the car etc.

KEEPING THE BALANCE

Too much hunting that always results in a retrieve can damage the quality of both behaviour chains. This applies particularly to the flushing dogs and HPR's. Only bring hunting and retrieving together in a balanced way otherwise the dog will self build a chain of a hunt that always ends in a retrieve. What we actually require is a hunt chain that ends with the drop to flush, pause, and then on your cue the retrieve chain.

Dogs learn from the job, this is natural learning. The more often a series of behaviours are repeated in the same order, the quicker the dog will learn the sequence. We utilise this skill to teach the dog cues, chains, and expect them to anticipate our teaching in many instances. But if you do not appreciate that this skill will be used without discrimination on all learning, you will effectively teach your dog to spend the day out with a free license to choose their own tasks, at their own time to suit their own pleasure.

Your dog will not be welcome on future shoots, and you may find yourself considering "quick fix" training methods to correct the dog, which have the habit of unfixing just as quickly. Investment of your time and energy from the start can prevent this from ever happening, and every extra minute spent in training will be evident on the shoot, with a demonstration of effortless partnership and a fulfiling and happy day out for both you and the dog.

RECIPE: 53

THE DIRECTED RETRIEVE

The success of this exercise will be dependent on the quality of your teaching in **SIT AND MARK** Recipe 44 *page 123*. If two dummies are placed, the one the dog should retrieve is the one they are set up to mark.

You will be teaching the dog the skill

▶   To only retrieve what they mark on your cue

▶   To sit straight alongside you

▶   Maintain focus on what they mark

1.   Begin by placing out two identical dummies, each of the same value, a good distance apart - 6 metres, let the dog watch you put them out and make sure they are in sight.

2.   Set yourself and the dog up so that you are facing the dummy you wish the dog to retrieve, cue the 'mark' and introduce a hand signal cue pointing in the right direction, when the dog looks at the correct dummy, click and reinforce with the retrieve.

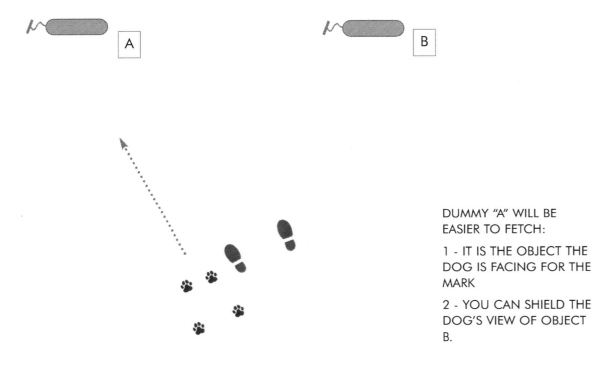

DUMMY "A" WILL BE EASIER TO FETCH:

1 - IT IS THE OBJECT THE DOG IS FACING FOR THE MARK

2 - YOU CAN SHIELD THE DOG'S VIEW OF OBJECT B.

3.   If the dog picks up the incorrect dummy, allow the retrieve to complete but lower the criteria by placing the chosen dummy closer so making it more attractive. Consolidate this skill then move on again.

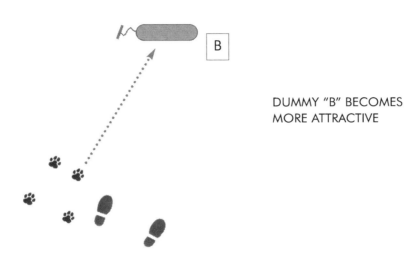

DUMMY "B" BECOMES
MORE ATTRACTIVE

4. Introduce rabbit dummy v plain dummy, clearly insight v partially hidden etc as simple steps, setting up the dog to succeed with the correct object placed in the easiest location. Consolidate each step, and ensure the dog does not begin to selectively retrieve "by object", only by your marked direction.

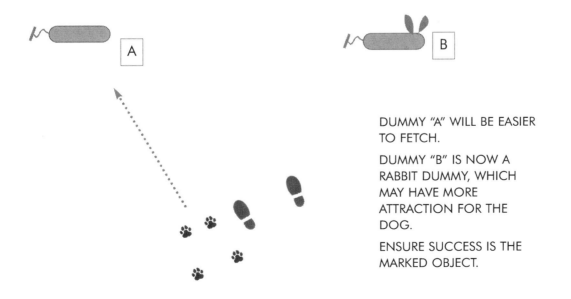

DUMMY "A" WILL BE EASIER TO FETCH.

DUMMY "B" IS NOW A RABBIT DUMMY, WHICH MAY HAVE MORE ATTRACTION FOR THE DOG.

ENSURE SUCCESS IS THE MARKED OBJECT.

RECIPE: 54

BLIND RETRIEVE

This is a combination of setting the dog up for a directed retrieve, sending them out in a straight line, letting their nose pick up the scent of the dummy or game which self cue the retrieve.

Start with the target work (*page 50*) for direction in Chapter 2 Foundation Training and the recipe for the **SIT AND MARK** Recipe 44 *page 123* linked with **DIRECTED RETRIEVE** Recipe 53 *page 139* for directed retrieve.

1. Send the dog out on the promise of reaching the target mat and substitute the mat for the dummy or game, which on sight will cue the pick up and following chain for retrieve. Click when the dog locates the dummy as the retrieve will then reinforce this.

2. Change to clicking for the straight out run, the scenting will then reinforce this, the dummy or game will then cue the retrieve which will self reinforce.

3. Increasing distance, including obstacles in the way, and hiding objects in more difficult places should be regarded as step by step increasing criteria. Introduce one at a time.

RECIPE: 55

RETRIEVE FROM WATER

Before introducing this skill the dog will need to have in place the skill of swimming and **SHAKING ON CUE** Recipe 8 *page 40* and a good retrieve .

A CAUTIONARY NOTE

Leave duck retrieval especially from water to the more experienced dog. Too much duck retrieval especially from strong flowing water may teach the inexperienced dog to hang on harder than needed with the effort of fighting the water, swimming and the desire not to let the capture escape. This may then transfer to all game, which is not desirable, and that will take some time to eradicate.

Begin with the light weight dummy that will float, this should have been included in your generalisation on the retrieve, make it more appealing by taking some dummy material and attaching it round the middle, tie a piece of light weight string to the end, just in case on the first couple of throws your dog struggles to make the connection (otherwise you will be getting wetter than you had planned).

Make sure you set the first attempts at the lowest criteria, close to the bank where it is easy for the dog to get out and the familiar location where they learnt to swim.

1. Set the dog up for the sit and mark, throw the dummy in to the water making sure the dog can see it and cue 'fetch', followed by the cue to enter the water click for entering the water, let the retrieve reinforce this, when the retrieve has been completed, pause then cue the dog to shake, click and let the dog self reinforce on the behaviour.

2. Then increase criteria gradually with weight first followed by texture, remember it is likely to be duck that your dog retrieves from water and they can be heavy. Then increase the distance from you to the water and the distance of the dummy in the water from the bank, and then finally so the dog is unable to see it.

RECIPE: 56

RETRIEVE OVER JUMP

Before you start, teach your dog to jump safely and confidently as an separate behaviour as in **JUMPING** Recipe 9 *page 42*, and the **BLIND RETRIEVE** Recipe 54 *page 142*.

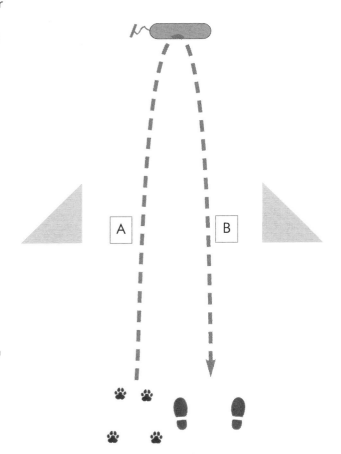

1. Begin by setting up the dog for a straight retrieve about 3 metres away from you. Repeat this pattern.

2. Then introduce the wings to the jump setting them up either side of the run to the dummy.

    Firstly, click the dog for going through them to retrieve (A). let the retrieve reinforce this click.

    Secondly, coming back to you through them (B). Both are decision points that you need to focus the dog's attention on.

4. Increase the distance from you to the wings and the wings to the dummy. Click the dog for the decision to come back through the wings.

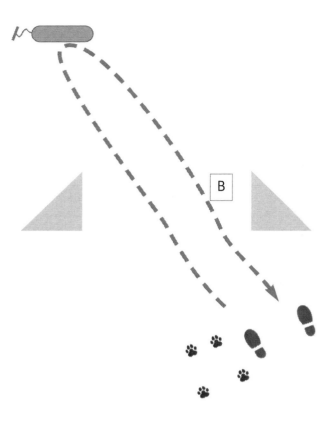

5. Change the angle you send the dog out from and again click for the decision to return through the wings (B). Consolidate this through various jump angles.

6. Then introduce a bar to the jump begin at the lowest level; introduce the cue to 'jump'. Make sure the dog can still see the dummy. Click for the jump on return.

7. Gradually increase the height to the maximum practical and safe for your dog. No extra marks for the dog that gets snagged on the barbed wire.

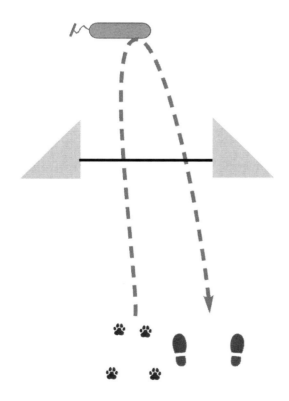

8. Then fill the jump in so the retrieve becomes blind, you hang a cloth over the bar. Cue the dog for each part of the chain, and then gradually reduce the cues from the back until the dog can do it on the 'fetch' cue.

POINT FOR DISCUSSION - HARD MOUTH IN DOGS

A dog can become hard mouthed from training, not just by genetic inheritance.

With clicker training our ability to teach clearly and with precision could potentially allow us to explain the preferred soft mouth carrying style.

I often equate this to the idea of the Collie who has been taught the skill to carry a raw egg while running and jumping and deliver it un-broken to hand. The Collie has no preconceptions of the hard mouth or the genetic inheritance of it, as is it also unaware of the soft mouth we so strongly equate to the gundogs. In fact during its development as the herding dog its point in the hunting chain was broken at the chase stage, the final stages eliminated with selective breeding. So if you can teach your dog to carefully manage a raw egg through the most difficult situations can you not teach your dog the skill of how hard to grip when carrying the game? High rate of reinforcement when the grip is firm but not hard, no damage, no reinforcement for too much pressure and damage.

High rate of reinforcement for unbroken egg, no reinforcement when broken - tries again.

6 Ready for the Shoot

BALANCE

As the teacher you are responsible for the quality of the dog's behaviours. If one behaviour breaks down then you will need to make a note and re-build it. Do not move on, until it is solid otherwise this behaviour will deteriorate further and will almost certainly bring down others with it.

Remember your dog is only doing what it perceives as the appropriate behaviour in those circumstances at that time. If this is not what you expect then you need to withdraw and go back to more training. You have not achieved a good balance between the desire to hunt and the ability to maintain self-control.

At the end of the day you are looking to improve your dog's field skill without reducing the willingness and happiness to carry out the tasks.

Continually vary the training programme. There is no fixed agenda to the order in which to teach your dog these skills. Begin with making sure the dog has had experience out in the hunting environment and gradually build through these skills. Alongside this I would be working through control exercises beginning in the least distracting location such as the kitchen.

This is the order I would move through what I consider to be the levels of environmental influence:

1. Kitchen

2. Garden

3. Field outside house

4. Outskirts of shoot, when not shooting

5. Wood at shoot, when not shooting

6. Next to pen at shoot, when not shooting

7. In pen at shoot, when not shooting

8. Outskirts of shoot on shoot day

If you are on a shoot day itself other than for allowing your dog the time to absorb the impact you should not be training. You should have in place all the skills you believe are required and at the level you expect them to be carried out. The shooting environment itself should be only used to gain experience for the dog.

The same is true for competition. Working tests are an excellent way of gaining experience for your dog. Field trials should only be entered if you feel your dog is ready to work for the gun. Go along to a few field trials and see what is expected this will give you a good base on which to set your expectations. Offering your services to a field trial secretary will often get you close enough to observe all the action.

The Kennel Club has commenced assessment on the working gundog tests. These have been designed to test whether a dog is ready to begin work in the shooting environment and a certificate of competence is issued if your dog passes. These are not competitions and each dog is assessed on their ability as opposed to against each other. This may be another way for you to assess if your dog is ready or not to take part in a day's shooting. The first level is under controlled conditions and does not involve game. The second stage you are assessed at a shoot of your choosing. The assessor comes to you at an agreed time and place and usually stays for the majority of the day. You can find information about this and competitions on The Kennel Club website.

The partnership you develop with your dog will begin right at the very start with your first training sessions. This is where you will need the skill to understand your dog and build the training programme to suit them. Always make sure that your criteria changes are achievable for your dog, your dogs success rate should be top priority. Make sure you give extra reward for effort and outstanding achievement.

If you have a young puppy that is already very strong in hunting, then you will need to move slowly through the hunting exercises and build more control work first. This is Rioja. The opposite is true if the puppy is very good at self-control then the hunting can be developed more quickly. This was Kemble.

Ask yourself the questions from Karen Pryor's *Don't Shoot the Dog* before moving on:

1. **Is it always the best?**

   Top quality only gets rewarded; never drop the standard once it is acheived, only the level.

2. **Will it always happen on cue?**

   You must be consistent with your cues and rewards for the understanding.

3. **Will happen anytime, anywhere, and anyplace.**

   Teach the dog to understand that the learning is always the same no matter what is happening or where it is.

4. **Will the behaviour happen when not cued?**

   Make sure you have not rewarded your dog for spontaneous behaviours.

Follow the following steps of learning and your training should naturally progress through to maintenance:

1. Break the behaviour down into small edible chunks

    a.   Make a plan how to teach

    b.   Make sure the dog has the fitness and skills needed

2. Get small behaviours to the top quality

3. Add your final cue, remember to save your whistle cues for this

4. Make sure the behaviour is then robust in all of the situations as anticipated stimulus increases

5. Begin to build your chains within the same contexts - retrieve, or hunting.

6. Delay reward from you - more for less - as the job will begin to be rewarding in its own right.

7. Then move into maintenance phase

    a.   Build confidence and experience

    b.   Introduce more puzzles to keep it fresh.

WORKING WALKS

These are very good ways of bringing all the skills together. Begin them in your lowest area of stimuli. Use them to develop

Matching pace	Stops	Drops
Recalls	Retrieves	Re-direction

Working at distance

Self control - 'watching the birds or rabbits go by'

Change the venues, gradually increasing the level of stimuli but making sure you never exceed your dog's level of success. Look for the signs that your dog is enjoying the work, if not, then take a look at your style of teaching. Perhaps you are expecting too much too soon or you have not introduced a high enough level of reward.

DOGGING IN

This activity is used to bring the young birds back towards the safety of the pen before the season commences and then continues during the season to keep the birds within the boundaries of the shoot.

It is an excellent way to teach the young dog the skills of hunting and self control in the future working environment. With the dog on a long line you can manage the situation.

Choose the times and manage the areas you work so that you do not exceed your dog's level of skill. The young dog will gain experience in moving the birds on without flushing, will learn how close to get, how to read the wind for scenting and you will be able to develop a good quartering pattern.

Make sure you get the keeper's permission first, the majority, once they know you are a responsible dog handler and will put the safety of the birds as priority, will welcome your help. You can also withdraw should things become too stimulating for the dog.

Remember hunting and retrieving are both powerful reinforcers. If your dog becomes too aroused stop the hunt and withdraw. Take your dog's pulse and breathing rates and wait for them to drop to what should be normal in this situation. Look for the signs of them becoming aware of you again, engage the lead as the cue for matching pace. Do not continue until the dog has regained self-control. Move to another area before you begin again.

PIGEON SHOOTING

Once your young dog has a solid retrieve on cold game, experience with the gun and you have begun to develop the sustained and self-control behaviours, then pigeon shooting is an ideal opportunity to bring them together and get experience in a working situation. The more pigeon shooting you can do the better.

Pigeon shooting is usually a very individual sport and because of this it makes it a great training situation for the dogs. I am not an expert on the sport, but the outline is:

The guns wait in some form of hide or at dusk when the birds are coming into roost. A number of 'decoys', plastic birds that look like pigeons, or more specialised looking birds on poles are placed out in an effort to look like a flock feeding. This encourages more pigeons to fly in.

Sitting in the hide with your dog waiting patiently for the birds to fly in is great for self-control. It also teaches them the skill of not reacting to the gun in a situation that is highly stimulating. They must remain quietly in the hide until sent for the bird otherwise the other pigeons will not fly in. Pigeons are very flighty and react to the slightest twitch or unusual look about the ground. You have a very high value reward to use in the retrieve. If you lay some shot birds out on the ground this also teaches the dog to discriminate between which birds to pick and which not. The ones with your scent on are to be left out the ones without your scent are to be collected.

I am not the best shot in the world and I think if it was me shooting pigeons as a training exercise for my dogs they would end up with great self-control but no retrieve skill! So under sufferance my husband volunteers to do the shooting part for me. Even if you don't shoot, engage the help of someone who does. Most avid pigeon shooters will gladly offer their services in return for not having to retrieve their own birds. There is always the offer of a free box of cartridges.

ALTERNATIVE CLICKS

Many people question how to use the clicker when the dogs are so far away.

The majority of the time if you have built your chains correctly and your dog also has a sound reinforcement history, the behaviours 'click' each other and the continuation of doing certain exercises in partnership with you is a long term click in itself.

You should also develop some other clicks for using out in the field.

Some examples are

▶   A hand click

▶   A tongue click

▶   A clap of the hands

▶   A particular word I use 'wow'

I know someone who, when working two dogs together, has conditioned a different word for each. He has found this very effective and each dog understands when they are being clicked.

The dogs' hearing is also very good and I have found that with a loud, box clicker they hear this quite adequately at some distance away. By the time they cannot hear it, you will have already conditioned some alternatives or if the dog is working that far away you should be using the behaviours to 'click' each other.

WORKING MORE THAN ONE DOG

As the bug for training takes a tighter hold, and the thrill of seeing them work in the field and take such great enjoyment from the sport, it is inevitable that the urge to have a second dog begins to develop.

Make sure that your behaviours are in place with both dogs before you begin to work them together. There will always be some natural competition which in itself is quite healthy. Watch and see how your dogs interact when not working and this will usually give you some idea how things will go when they are out together. I have found that some dogs are natural at taking the lead and the others slot well into the team with them. The roles will vary as the tasks change. My girls are the better hunters on scent but the boy is the stronger retriever. He will often defer to the girls when hunting and take their lead but then on retrieves they will defer to him unless there is more than one. I have observed that they are also very good at developing skill within each other and if a behaviour is strong in one dog you can use this to teach the other.

Although there is not data yet to prove this I am convinced that the dogs learn extremely well by observing each other work. I can be teaching a behaviour in the kitchen with one dog while the others watch. When this dog has finished and I swap over often the second dog will immediately offer the behaviour I had just been teaching. I use this as often as I can when out with the dogs. The older ones actively teach the younger ones for me.

Backing is a term used for the HPR's. It is where one dog will honour the point of another. So when working out in the field if one dog comes up to point, then the second dog will not run up but take up a deferred position on the scent. The flush is given to the first dog. I have seen all four of my dogs do this, each one deferring to the one before them on the scent. You can develop this skill using the clicker. In my experience once the dogs have good sound skills in place this will naturally evolve and becomes a solid behaviour with experience.

Experience will teach your dog a lot of things that you may not have thought would be required. For example, I am right handed and lift the gun to my right shoulder. I have taught the dogs to work from my left. My husband is left-handed and lifts the gun to his left shoulder. I have not taught the dogs to change sides, neither has he. But Thorn, from experience with my husband, positions himself on his right, slightly further out than with me so he can have a good view ready to mark the birds when shot. With me, he takes up position on the left. The young girl has now begun to do exactly the same.

This to me is the 'essence' of a clicker trained dog and the trust between partners.

Have fun and enjoy the sport.

Appendix A - Glossary

Acknowledge scent

the dog recognise the scent of the game and focus on it.

Air Scent   for the purposes of this book is scent coming from the body of game that rises in wafts of small particles then carried on the wind.

Back casting   where the dog turns down wind and begins to recover the ground that has already been worked.

Backing   a term used for the Hunt Point Retrieve breeds, where one dog will honour the point of another.

Beating   walking and working dogs through a selected area rousing game forward towards a line of guns.

Beat/Beating Line

the selected area for rousing game; often refers to the area between each beater when working in a line. It is also the selected area for a dog to quarter. This will vary depending on the type of dog. A specifically defined area in rough shooting, tests or trials. The distance of a beat is greater for Hunt Point Retrieve breeds than for flushing dogs.

Beater   person responsible for rousing game for the guns.

Bevy   group of quail.

Blank firing pistol

small hand help pistol fires caps and simulates the sound of gun shot.

Blinking   where the hunting dog locates the game but fails to acknowledge it either by flushing, pointing or working up to the game, the dog will often turn away just before reaching the game.

Bolting rabbit   green canvas dummy attached to a long length of strong elastic used to simulate a rabbit bolting from cover.

Boring into the wind

is where the dog encounters large amounts of ground scent, stops quartering and follows this instead, at the end of the scent pool the dog begins to quarter again.

Bundle of wings   these can be any variety including pheasants, partridge, duck. Cut from the bird when fresh.

Caged bird   game bird kept in a special cage used to provide scent for hunt training or the flush for drop training.

Cast   where the dog is set out in decisive pattern (quartering).

Cold game   game shot and stored intact.

Commercial shoot

large organised shoots run for profit. Guns pay to attend.

DEFRA   Department for Environment, Food and Rural Affair.

Dizzying   to "hypnotise" a pigeon see page 107 for explanation.

Dogging in   where the dogs are used to bring the young birds back towards the safety of the pen before the season commences and then continues during the season to keep the birds within the boundaries of the shoot.

Drive   the area selected for the beaters to

work at rousing the game, the game is driven towards the guns some shoots are called 'driven shoots'.

Dummy   canvas bag filled with sand comes in a variety of weights to teach the dog retrieve, most common is green.

Dummy launcher
                    piece of equipment designed to be fired using blanks and launches a dummy into the air whilst making a noise 'similar' to gun shot.

Flush   cause the birds to take to wing and fly away.

Flushing dogs   the breeds of dogs, including spaniels, that quarter across the wind on a close beat of apporximately 15 yds (5m) holding their head low. The distance was based on half the average range of a shotgun. When the scent is located they run around busily until the game is flushed. They are not expected to stop still on the scent of game.

Ground Scent   scent retained by the soil or vegetation that game has been in contact with.

Gun/Guns   person who carries a gun and shoots the game on the day or the instrument that shoots the game.

Hunt Point Retrievers (HPRs)
                    the breeds of dogs that use air scent to locate the game carry their heads at shoulder height, dipping or lowering their heads as they 'taste' the air. They quarter a much greater beat to the flushing dogs simply because of the development of the pointing behaviour. The ability to remain still on the location of game until the guns can be placed in position, they will also include the pointer and setters.

Keeper   person who looks after the ground and game, feeding, watering, pest control and organising which areas are to be shot on which days, running the beaters and beating lines, supervising the pickers up.

Picking up   the dogs working behind the line of guns retrieving all shot game.

Pickers up   people responsible for retrieving the shot game.

Placed   as in dummies, game or birds, this is where you actually position them in specific places that you can re-locate later.

Poaching   illegal catching of game.

Priest   weighted heavy small truncheon like instrument designed to despatch game effieciently and be easy to carry.

Quail   small bird of partridge family.

Quarry/Game -   these are often referred to as the same but game does not include pests such as squirrel, rabbits and pigeon.

Quartering   dog runs to and fro whilst advancing in an up wind direction. The distance is usually specified by the beat.

Quest   to search.

Retrievers   the breeds of dogs responsible for locating and retrieving shot game. *See page 3.*

Rough Shooting working mainly on a one to one basis with your dogs and a gun. Dogs find, flush and retrieve the game that has been successfully shot.

Running in   the dog does not maintain the flush and runs in as soon as it scents the game.

Scent   how the dogs track by smell and detect the presence of game, the odours that the game gives off, either on the ground or rising from their bodies into the air. Can be puchased in a bottle.

Scented dummy   dummy artificially impregnated with natural scent of game.

Stickiness   the dog holds onto the point and does not move into flush on cue.

Strike   when the dog is quartering and hits the cone of scent from game.

Syndicate Shoot   privately run shoot by a group of guns.

Tame game   game that is fed, watered. General welfare is managed.

Using the wind   working the dog into the wind to help maximise the success of finding the scent.

Warm game   game just shot.

Wild game   game that is free to come and go as it pleases although food and water may be provided in strategic places.

Winding   dog locates the game by scent not having been aware of its location before.

Wing   one cut from any game bird.

With the wind the wind is blowing into your face and the dog will work from right to left across you into the wind, often referred to as heading into the wind

With a cheek wind

the wind is blowing onto your cheek and the dog still quarters with the wind.

With a tail wind   the wind is blowing from behind you and the dog will be sent out in a straight line and will quarter back towards you

With a side wind the wind is blowing from the side of you the dog will be sent out in a straight line down wind and quarter back into the wind across you.

Appendix B

QUESTIONNAIRE FOR MEASURING THE EFFECT OF STIMULI

Stimulus under test [   ]   Intensity   High   Medium   Low

Dog [   ]   Age [   ]

Location [   ]   Date [   ]

                                                                                    points

1. PROXIMITY   a. Is the dog aware you are there   Y / N   _____

                          b. Is the dog aware you are missing   Y / N   _____

Yes to both scores 1, Yes to a. No to b. scores 2, No to both scores 3

2. FOCUS   a. Is the dog outwardly focused and unable
                             to look at you at all   Y / N   _____

                          b. Can the dog be lured to look at you   Y / N   _____

                          c. Is the dog able to look at you   Y / N   _____

Yes to a. scores 3, Yes to b. scores 2, Yes to c. scores 1

3. NOISE   a. Does the dog bark and whine constantly Y / N   _____

                          b. Persistent whining   Y / N   _____

                          c. Intermittent whine   Y / N   _____

                          d. No noise from the dog   Y / N   _____

Yes to a. scores 3, Yes to b. scores 2, Yes to c. scores 1, Yes to d. scores 0

4. MOVEMENT   a. Does the dog throw about at the
                             end of the lead   Y / N   _____

                          b. Consistently fidget   Y / N   _____

                          c. Slight movement   Y / N   _____

                          d. No movement   Y / N   _____

Yes to a. scores 3, Yes to b. scores 2, Yes to c. scores 3, yes to d. scores 0

5. SENSITIVITY TO TOUCH

                          a. No response to finger push on thigh   Y / N   _____

b. Slight give in movement but
no acknowledgement   Y / N   _____

c. Acknowledgement and movement away   Y / N   _____

d. Complete focus on you on finger push   Y / N   _____

Yes to a. scores 3, Yes to b. scores 2, Yes to c. scores 1, Yes to d. scores 0

6. SIGHT BLOCKING

a. Agitates dog, tries to remove block, bites etc. Y / N   _____

b. Frustrates dog but does not
physically try to move it   Y / N   _____

c. Only slight frustration - looking round it   Y / N   _____

d. Not bothered   Y / N   _____

Yes to a. scores 3, Yes to b. scores 2, Yes to c. scores 1, Yes to d. scores 0

7. EATING FOOD

a. Can the dog eat food in presence
of the stimulus   Y / N   _____

If No then: b. Can the dog eat food when the distance
is increased away from the stimulus   Y / N   _____

c. Can the dog eat food when the stimulus
is removed completely   Y / N   _____

Yes to a. scores 0, Yes to b. scores 5, Yes to c. scores 10

8. RESPONSE TO CUE

a. No response to cue   Y / N   _____

b. Responds to cue but unable to look at you   Y / N   _____

c. Responds and looks   Y / N   _____

d. Dog is focussed on you at the start
and immediate response   Y / N   _____

Yes to a. scores 3, Yes to b. scores 2, Yes to c scores 1, Yes to d. scores 0

Score:	31	28	25	22	19	16	13	10	7	4	2
Stimulus level:	10	9	8	7	6	5	4	3	2	1	0

MEASURING BEHAVIOUR

Behaviour under test

Dog

Age

Location

Date

Reward ratio   1:1

No of repetitions					
1					
2					
3					
4					
5					
6					
7					
8					
9					
10					
% Success at 3					

Stimulus level 1

Stimulus level 2

Stimulus level 3

Stimulus level 4

Stimulus level 5

Behaviour:
0 = does not happen
1 = weak in both memory and physical skill
2 = weak in either memory or physical skill
3 = strong in both memory and physical skill